Othello JAMES EARL

Internationally known for his theatre, television and film performances, James Earl Jones has played Othello seven times during his career. He was twenty-five when he first played Othello in summer stock theatre in Michigan. He last undertook the role on Broadway in 1981, when he was fifty. His long association with the land-mark New York Shakespeare Festival began in 1959, and led to roles in *Hamlet, King Lear, The Merchant of Venice, The Tempest, Macbeth* and others. His 1964 performance in *Othello* garnered a Drama Desk Award for Best Performance by an Actor. His first Tony Award came for his starring role in *The Great White Hope* in 1969, and he won a second Tony Award in 1987 for his work in August Wilson's *Fences*.

His film work includes *Cry, the Beloved Country, A Family Thing, Field of Dreams, Matewan*, the first three Star Wars movies, the first three Tom Clancy movies and *The Lion King*. He won an Emmy Award for Best Actor in a Drama Series for his lead role in the television series, *Gabriel's Fire*, and has received many other awards and honours, including a tribute in the 2002 Kennedy Center Honors in Washington, DC.

James Earl Jones's autobiography, *Voices and Silences*, co-authored with Penelope Niven, was published in 2001.

Colin Nicholson is the originator and editor for the *Actors on Shakespeare* series published by Faber and Faber.

JAMES EARL JONES

Othello

Series Editor: Colin Nicholson

faber and faber

First published in 2003
by Faber and Faber Limited
3 Queen Square London WC1N 3AU

Typeset by Faber and Faber in Minion
Printed in England by Mackays of Chatham, plc

The right of James Earl Jones to be identified as author of this work has
been asserted in accordance with Section 77 of the Copyright, Designs
and Patents Act 1988

The right of Colin Nicholson to be identified as author of the introduc-
tion has been asserted in accordance with Section 77 of the Copyright,
Designs and Patents Act 1988

*This book is sold subject to the condition that it shall not, by way of trade
or otherwise, be lent, resold, hired out or otherwise circulated without the
publisher's prior consent in any form of binding or cover other than that
in which it is published and without a similar condition including this
condition being imposed on the subsequent purchaser*

A CIP record for this book
is available from the British Library

ISBN 0–571–21675–7

10 9 8 7 6 5 4 3 2 1

Introduction

Shakespeare: Playwright, Actor and Actors' Playwright

It is important to remember that William Shakespeare was an actor, and his understanding of the demands and rewards of acting helped him as a playwright to create roles of such richness and depth that actors in succeeding generations – even those with no reason or desire to call themselves 'classical' actors – have sought opportunities to perform them.

As the company dramatist, Shakespeare was writing under the pressure of producing scripts for almost immediate performance by his fellow players – the Lord Chamberlain's Men (later the King's Men), who, as a share-holding group, had a vested interest in their playhouse. Shakespeare was writing for a familiar set of actors: creating roles for particular players to interpret; and, being involved in a commercial enterprise, he was sensitive to the direct contact between player and audience and its power to bring in paying customers. His answer to the challenge produced a theatrical transformation: Shakespeare peopled the stage with highly credible personalities, men and women who were capable of change, and recognizable as participants in the human condition which their audience also shared. He connected two new and important elements: the idea of genuine individuality – the solitary, reflecting, self-communing soul, which is acutely aware of its own sufferings and desires; and, correlatively, the idea of inner life as something that not only exists but can also be explored. For him, the connection became the motor of dramatic action on the stage, as it is the motor of personal action in real life.

The primary importance of the actor cannot be disputed: it is his or her obligation – assisted to a greater or lesser extent by a director's overall vision of the play – to understand the personality they are representing onstage and the nature of the frictions taking place when that personality interacts with other characters in the drama: Shakespeare's achievement goes far beyond the creation of memorable characters (Macbeth, Falstaff) to embrace the exposition of great relationships (Macbeth–Lady Macbeth; Falstaff–Prince Hal). Great roles require great actors, and there is no group of people in a better position to interpret those roles to *us* than the principal actors of *our* generation – inhabitants of a bloodline whose vigour resonates from the sixteenth century to the present day – who have immersed themselves in the details of Shakespeare's creations and have been party to their development through rehearsal and performance.

Watching Shakespeare can be an intimidating experience, especially for those who are not well versed in the text, or in the conventions of the Elizabethan stage. Many excellent books have been written for the academic market but our aim in this series is somewhat different. *Actors on Shakespeare* asks contemporary performers to choose a play of particular interest to them, push back any formal boundaries that may obstruct channels of free communication and give the modern audience a fresh, personal view. Naturally the focus for each performer is different – and these diverse volumes are anything but uniform in their approach to the task – but their common intention is, primarily, to look again at plays that some audiences may know well and others not at all, as well as providing an insight into the making of a performance.

Each volume works in its own right, without assuming an in-depth knowledge of the play, and uses substantial quotation to contextualize the principal points. The fresh approach of the many and varied writers will, we hope, enhance your enjoyment of Shakespeare's work.

Colin Nicholson
February 2002

Note: For reference, the text used here is
the Arden Shakespeare.

Characters

Othello, *a noble Moor in the service of the Venetian State*
Brabantio, *a Senator of Venice and Desdemona's father*
Cassio, *Othello's Lieutenant*
Iago, *Othello's Ancient*
Roderigo, *a Venetian Gentleman*
Duke of Venice
Other Senators
Montano, *Othello's predecessor in the government of Cyprus*
Gratiano, *Brother of Brabantio*
Lodovico, *Kinsman of Brabantio*
Clown, Servant to Othello
Desdemona, *Brabantio's daughter and Othello's wife*
Emilia, *Iago's wife*
Bianca, *a Courtesan*
Sailor, Messenger, Herald, Officers, Gentlemen, Musicians and Attendants

Othello was performed at the Winter Garden Theatre in New York in 1982, with the following cast:

Othello	James Earl Jones
Iago	Christopher Plummer
Desdemona	Cecilia Hart (replacing Dianne Wiest)
The Duke, Montano	Robert Burr
Cassio	Kelsey Grammer
Roderigo	Stephen Markle
Emilia	Aideen O'Kelly
Brabantio	David Sabin
Lodovico	Raymond Skipp
Servant, Cypriot	Kim Ameen
Herald, Soldier	Kim Bemis
Gentleman, Officer	Dan Desmond
Gratiano	Richard Dix
Servant, Cypriot	Randy Kovitz
Senator, Gentleman, Servant, Officer	Edwin McDonough
Bianca	Ellen Newman
Gentleman, Servant	Bern Sundstedt
Director	Peter Coe
Scenic Design	David Chapman
Costumes	Robert Fletcher
Lighting Design	Marc B. Weiss
Producers	Barry and Fran Weissler

That is what we do to the work of the dramatist, we bring to life what is hidden under the words . . .

Stanislavski, *An Actor Prepares*

To students and actors
who are discovering
Shakespeare's 'mighty magic'
for themselves

Acknowledgements

The following people have provided invaluable assistance during the journey of this book:

My wife, Cecilia Hart Jones; Coddy Granum and Fionna Feehan of Horatio Productions; my editor in London, Colin Nicholson; my editor and colleague in the United States, Penelope Niven.

I also salute my fellow writers in this series, for their perspectives on Shakespeare.

James Earl Jones

Foreword

In 1964, at the age of thirty-three, James Earl Jones won an Obie award for his off-Broadway portrayal of Othello in Joseph Papp's production in Central Park, New York. That same year, at the Old Vic in London, Laurence Olivier gave his much-celebrated performance in the role for the National Theatre. Critic Tom Prideaux, writing in *Life* magazine, pronounced the legendary Olivier's Othello 'justly celebrated' and the newcomer Jones's 'unjustly neglected'. He found Jones's performance 'immensely moving'.[*]

James Earl Jones has played the role seven times at different stages in his life and, therefore, his Othello has evolved with time and experience. When he appeared as Othello in Los Angeles in 1971, he observed, 'You have to start working on the part when you're young so that you can work up to a full comprehension of the man.'

Jones's 1981–2 performance (from Stratford, Connecticut, to Broadway) was deemed definitive, masterly, magnificent. Drama critic Clive Barnes admired his voice and his 'statuesque nobility', and praised Jones and Christopher Plummer, as Iago, for 'acting of great stature and brilliant imagination'.[†] Some critics have hailed Jones as the greatest American Othello: John Simon called him 'the best American Othello I am aware of, Paul Robeson's not excluded'.[††] Christine Arnold wrote that she and others believed that 'Jones has evolved into the greatest American Othello. Some say he has surpassed Paul

[*] Tom Prideaux, *Life* magazine, 11 December 1964.
[†] Clive Barnes, 'It's a Noble "Othello"', *New York Post*, 4 February 1982.
[††] John Simon, *New York*, 7 September 1981.

Robeson, whose 1944 *Othello* with Jose Ferrer and Uta Hagen set the standard. Until now.'*

Jones's deep study and contemplation of the role offstage undergirds his brilliance and majesty as Othello onstage. This long preoccupation with Othello is demonstrated in an incident reported by Elin Schoen in the *New York Times*, 31 January 1982: a fan approached James Earl Jones, saying, 'I know you!' and searching for a name, then said, 'You're . . . you're Othello!'

'Not quite,' Jones replied with a smile. 'But I'm getting there.'

In this book, James Earl Jones shares his quest to solve the mystery of the Moor.

* Christine Arnold, *Philadelphia Inquirer*, 30 December 1981.

'Little Otto'

I have always taken *Othello* personally – perhaps too personally – and I am not alone. Therefore this book is a personal exploration of *Othello* the play, of Othello the man, and of the other human beings who inhabit Shakespeare's Venice and his Cyprus. I'll also take a journey back into productions of *Othello* that have figured in my own life because I have seen them, read or heard about them, or performed in them. Finally, I'll examine some perspectives from others who have taken *Othello* personally, too.

I have heard the legend of a nineteenth-century road company playing *Othello* in a tour through small towns in the American West. One night, back in the era of the flamboyant American outlaw Belle Starr, they performed in a theatre house in one of the mountain states. Those old gas footlights lit the stage where Iago was doing his dirty work. Suddenly, somebody in the audience pulled out a gun and shot him. The sheriff asked the man why he did it. 'Well,' he answered, 'Iago was up to no good. He was a dastardly evil villain and I just had to shoot him.' Now, *there* was a man who took *Othello* a little too personally.

On the other hand, a positive interaction with *Othello* can be a good thing. It can make you attentive to the actor's task, which is to commit to the revelation of the characters, and thereby to help articulate the themes and issues in this majestic mountain of a play. It can make you think deeply about the personal and universal significance of the drama.

Othello and this play interlock to form a puzzle that has intrigued actors, directors and audiences across four centuries.

I confess that *Othello* the play is still a mystery to me, and I am content that it always will be. It is the mystery of it that makes the mountain interesting. I have played Othello in seven productions over twenty-five years, and studied and thought about the character and the play for many more years than that. I was twenty-five when I first tried to step into Othello's skin in, of all places, a summer stock theatre in Manistee, Michigan. I was fifty when I last took up the challenge, this time in a production that opened at the Shakespeare Festival in Stratford, Connecticut in 1981, and eventually, on 3 February 1982, dragged itself onto the Winter Garden stage in New York. I want to explore what I have learned and what I am still learning about *Othello*, in the event that something may be worth passing on. All of this has to do with how to get the play off the page and onto the stage, with as much allegiance as possible to the integrity of the play. Only then can you give the drama its full magnitude.

William Shakespeare was a great adaptor. For *Othello*, he drew on Giraldi Cinthio's *Hecatommithi* (1565). In turn, when Cinthio composed his collection of love stories, he was influenced by Boccaccio's *Decameron*. Cinthio wrote a hundred and ten stories in his series of romances – an introductory set of ten, and then ten 'decades' of ten stories each. In the third 'decade', Cinthio examined marital infidelity. Story seven in the third decade contains the following lines. As you read them, imagine yourself to be Will Shakespeare, looking for characters and a plot for a new play:

> There was once in Venice a Moor, a very gallant man,
> who . . . was personally valiant and had given proof in
> warfare of great prudence and skilful energy . . . It
> happened that a virtuous Lady of wondrous beauty called
> Disdemona, impelled not by female appetite but by the

Moor's good qualities, fell in love with him, and he, vanquished by the Lady's beauty and noble mind, likewise was enamoured of her ... They were united in marriage and lived together in such concord and tranquillity while they remained in Venice, that never a word passed between them that was not loving ... The Moor had in his company an Ensign of handsome presence but the most scoundrelly nature in the world. He was in high favour with the Moor, who had no suspicion of his wickedness; for although he had the basest of minds, he so cloaked the vileness hidden in his heart with high sounding and noble words, and by his manner, that he showed himself in the likeness of a Hector or an Achilles ...

With those lines, Cinthio introduced his reader to three unusual characters in very partisan tones. Shakespeare was bent on transforming a rather straightforward but essentially melodramatic tale into a drama worthy to be classified among his tragedies. I am grateful to Cinthio for the genesis of three great characters, but in Iago's case I beg the reader not to think of Iago in 'scoundrelly' terms. Hear him out. I will do my best not to perpetrate the label 'scoundrel', because I do not want to perpetuate that image of Iago. Let's not settle for the interpretation that is too easy. Let's not shoot Iago before we have heard him out.

Cinthio's story, like Shakespeare's, tells of intrigue and a handkerchief, and fires of suspicion, kindled to an inferno in the Moor by the Ensign until all the principal characters are consumed and destroyed, including the 'virtuous Lady of wondrous beauty'. Cinthio's Moor and his Ensign beat Disdemona to death with a stocking filled with sand, and then conspire to make the death appear to be an accident. Once their deed is discovered, Cinthio's Moor is tortured and then condemned to exile, an exile that ends when Disdemona's relatives kill him. The Ensign is arrested and tortured 'so fiercely that his inner organs were ruptured'. Let out of prison, he dies 'miserably' at home.

'Thus,' Cinthio concludes, 'did God avenge the innocence of Disdemona. And all these events were told after his death by the Ensign's wife, who knew the facts as I have told them to you.'*

Shakespeare named his gallant Moor 'Othello', and called his play *The Tragedy of Othello, the Moor of Venice*. One conjecture about the source of this name, which was unusual in Shakespeare's time, is that Shakespeare may have been drawing on 'Othoman', a variant spelling of 'Ottoman'.† Othello can be the diminutive of Otto, as in 'Ottoman Empire': Little Otto.

Disdemona – the dis-demon or anti-demon – became Desdemona, a woman of strength as well as beauty and virtue. Cinthio's Ensign was transformed into a complicated human being called Iago. It has been noted that there was a Sant' Iago, Saint James of Compostella, who was called 'Matamoros', or the 'Moor-killer'.†† (Certainly Iago, in doing the state and his general some service, became a 'Turk-killer'.) Shakespeare's Iago is not simply a narrow, one-dimensional villain or a symbol of some ethical order. He is a functioning human being, just as Othello and Desdemona are. His negative qualities are rooted in a history of powerlessness and deprivation. In the culture where Shakespeare has situated Iago, there was not much future for a smart, ambitious person who was powerless. Iago (called the ancient, or the ensign) worked for Othello, the general, in a very particular way. Far more than a standard-bearer, as the label 'ensign' suggests, he was a trouble-shooter,

* E. A. J. Honigmann, editor, *The Arden Shakespeare: Othello* (London: Thomson Learning, Berkshire House, 2001), 371–87.
† See Honigmann, 334.
†† See Honigmann, 334.

Othello's eyes and ears, and an agent. At best, Iago could rationalize his actions in the play by saying, 'I did what I did because it was my job. It was my job to test everybody. It was my job to spy. It was my job to play devil's advocate.'

Using the scaffolding of Cinthio's story, Shakespeare shaped his own characters and built this haunting and often enigmatic drama that he wrote most likely just after *Hamlet* and just before *King Lear*.[*] The bare bones of the plot hint of melodrama: Othello is a noble Moor, a general in the service of Venice. His ensign, Iago, is disappointed and angry when Othello passes him over to appoint Michael Cassio as his lieutenant. Iago sets out to avenge Othello's 'oversight'.

Othello has eloped with Desdemona, daughter of Brabantio, a Venetian senator. Iago inflames Brabantio by insinuating that Othello has kidnapped and dishonoured his daughter. Othello defends himself before the Duke and the Senate, and then goes off to war in Cyprus. His bride also speaks forthrightly to the Duke and to her father about her love for Othello, and goes to Cyprus as well. There, Iago engineers Cassio's disgrace and dismissal, and then hints to Othello that Desdemona and Cassio have had an intimate relationship. He offers 'proof', including the handkerchief Othello has given Desdemona: Iago's own wife Emilia finds the handkerchief and entrusts it to Iago, who plants it with Cassio.

Iago persists in his 'temptation' of Othello. Othello's confusion and disbelief mount until he strangles the innocent Desdemona. After Desdemona is killed, Emilia acknowledges Iago's actions – too late – and denounces them. Iago kills Emilia. Realizing that he has thrown away a pearl 'richer than all his tribe', Othello commits suicide, and Iago is condemned to torture.

[*] See Honigmann, 1, among many others.

But there is far more to this story than melodrama. Othello, Desdemona and Iago stand like three pillars supporting the drama, and each of them possesses mythic qualities. Othello comes from the same mythic worlds that Beowulf and Ulysses came out of. The spiritual 'visage' of Othello attracts the good angel and 'fair warrior' Desdemona. Iago is a Lucifer, the beautiful fallen angel, and he refers to himself as Janus.

The play is about the metamorphosis of the character of Othello and, to a great extent, the metamorphosis of the character of Iago. It is also about the unravelling of these characters. There are love and hate in both cases. Pure love exists in Othello and Desdemona. There is psychotic or schizophrenic love with Iago, but passion just as strong, just as powerful.

When we try to define Iago as Othello's agent, it seems to me we begin to fathom one of the themes in the play. If you were to integrate Iago into Othello, you would give Othello extra eyes and ears. We are talking about unity and dis-integration; unity and disunity. Othello and Desdemona share a cosmic unity and they are compelled to come together. Othello and Iago share a career unity, and their unity is the first to exist in the play.

It has been suggested that in Venice Othello was never quite whole without Iago. I want to define Iago as a part of Othello. Before you find fault with Iago, you have to know that he was trained by Othello. He was commissioned by Othello to do the agenting, the trouble-shooting, the spying.

Othello certainly is not whole without Desdemona. In a way, one unity displaces the other. Once Othello finds his fulfilment with Desdemona, that sours and weakens his unity with Iago; and Othello has further diminished that unity by choosing Cassio over Iago. We can probably find this paradox of unity and disunity running throughout the whole play. Chaos is a wonderfully dramatic counter to unity, but the more direct, organic opposite of unity is disunity or dis-integration. The tragedy in this play might be viewed as the progressive disunity or dis-integration of Othello and Iago.

I think we can say that one definition of the hero in this play is that he is out of joint with time. This is true of Othello, of Desdemona and of Cassio. In Othello's case, he is out of joint with place as well. Perhaps it is valid to look at this disjointedness against the backdrop of the Elizabethan sense of order: 'the great chain of being', where everyone and everything occupied a certain place or held a certain degree in a 'fixed and permanent system of ascending values'.* The chain of being specifically accounted for the rank and order of angels in the heavens, human beings on earth, clerics in the church, family members in the home, animals in the kingdom, fish in the sea, trees in the forest. The Elizabethan playwright entertaining and edifying the Elizabethan audience could transplant that deeply ingrained chain of being to Venice or Cyprus, and test the waters there when certain hierarchies of relationship and behaviour were violated. In fact, there could be more freedom in testing controversial waters in a drama set in a foreign place – Venice or Cyprus – rather than in London.

Given this view of the divinely ordered universe, the properly ordered society and the traditionally structured family, it is no wonder that Brabantio was appalled when his daughter married Othello without his permission. This was a profound violation of family order, all other issues aside. No wonder that Othello cashiered Cassio for his drunken display, which was a breach of military order, unbefitting an officer of his rank and station. As the drama of *Othello* unfolds, relationships

* William G. Leary, *Shakespeare Plain: The Making and Performing of Shakespeare's Plays* (New York: McGraw-Hill Book Company, 1977), 256–7.

rupture before our eyes into disharmony and disunity: Roderigo and Iago; Brabantio and Desdemona; Iago and Cassio; Iago and Emilia; Desdemona and Othello.

As William G. Leary has written of the Elizabethan world, 'The principle of hierarchical organization was discovered in all human institutions. Hence, in a kingdom, the monarch was God's steward, and all groups, ranks, and classes in society owed him unswerving allegiance. What the king was to his nation the father was to his family. And the order in the universe had to serve as the model for the order that every right-thinking person sought to impose on his own conduct.'*

Disunity, disharmony, disorder, and disobedience dictate consequences and conflict – the stuff drama is made of.

---

* Leary, 256.

Othello the Moor

> Here is the man, this Moor, whom now it seems
> Your special mandate, for the state-affairs,
> Hath hither brought.
>> Brabantio to the Duke (Act I, scene iii)

Over the years, I have seen a mosaic of Othello's life based on references in the text. He seems to have been of noble birth, a prince of a Muslim kingdom, probably in North Africa. His name, as I have said, may have been a diminutive of Otto: Little Otto. This evokes for me the child Othello, before the prince, and certainly before the warrior. Othello the vulnerable human being, hopeful about the future. This is a strong element in the play.

Othello is defined by his culture rather than his colour. He was raised in wealth and stature in a Moorish court. Therefore one layer of his psyche is accustomed to privilege; unlike Iago, Othello is not aware of what it means to be a 'second-class citizen'. Othello's early days were not those of a Westernized African man vulnerable to colonialism and slavery. Skin colour has been stigmatized by slavery, and that blurs what being 'black' is and was. The Westernized African man would have been both keenly aware and also unconsciously aware of the stigma of the second-class citizen. Therefore he would have been socially guarded. As a prince, Othello had no such experience and awareness. As a prince, he became a warrior, and as a warrior, he was taken prisoner and sold to slavery, a slavery that did not reduce his noble nature, but in some ways enriched it by widening his consciousness.

He tells us some of this when he is called before the Duke and the senators to explain his relationship to Desdemona:

> Her father lov'd me, oft invited me,
> Still question'd me the story of my life,
> From year to year; the battles, sieges, fortunes,
> That I have pass'd:
> I ran it through, even from my boyish days,
> To the very moment that he bade me tell it.
> Wherein I spake of most disastrous chances,
> Of moving accidents by flood and field;
> Of hair-breadth scapes i' th' imminent deadly breach;
> Of being taken by the insolent foe;
> And sold to slavery; of my redemption thence,
> And with it all my travel's history . . .
> (Act I, scene iii)

It also appears that, at some point between his birth and the time the play opens, Othello has converted to Catholicism. When in Venice, pray as the Venetians do. He has seemingly abandoned his Islamic faith. That probably can be accounted for during the part of his life spent in slavery. He became antagonistic toward those non-Christians who captured him and sold him. The Christian world, he felt, was friendlier. When the Moors conquered and captured, they would absorb the conquered males into the Moorish army, often giving them very responsible positions. They were more interested in integrating them than in enslaving them. Othello, being accustomed to that tradition, would have a harder time with the Turks, who did not do it that way. The Turkish armies were very strong at that time, and far more ruthless in conquest than the Moors. Othello became, with his 'Matamoros' ensign, 'Sant' Iago', an expert at killing the Turks, 'the Ottomites', the enemies of the Venetians. That's why the Venetians hired him.

He is a Moor, now in service to the Duke of Venice as a general in the Venetian army and as the governor of Cyprus.

Othello's native language is Arabic, and I assume that he speaks Spanish. The Islamic people had conquered Spain in the eighth century, and the conquering people would speak the language of the conquered. As a general in the Venetian army, Othello surely speaks Italian, but it is a new language for him.

We have to take into account at least three cultural layers in order to understand Othello. First, there is his high birth. Next, there is his low existence as a slave and his chaotic existence as a warrior. As we shall see, the word 'chaos' (disintegration) is key to his whole tragedy. It is the opposite of unity. Finally, there is paradise. Othello finds paradise again when he finds love and peace with Desdemona.

He has wooed and married Desdemona, daughter of a Venetian senator. Othello envisions a new life with Desdemona. Unfortunately, unbeknownst to him, Iago, his trusted ensign, seeks to sabotage Othello's marriage. Because Othello trusts Iago implicitly, Iago is particularly subversive.

Othello relies on Iago for many services, one of them as an interpreter of Venetian culture. Othello is essentially a stranger in a strange land – a sophisticated, cosmopolitan, cultured man who is removed from his own world. This noble Moor is set apart from his soldiers and from the Venetian court by his culture. As a foreigner, he relies on Iago to help him understand the social and political world of Venice, as well as the warrior world of Cyprus. Othello also trusts Iago as the military subordinate who keeps an eye on details for him; Iago most likely functions like an aide-de-camp, handling security and intelligence matters for his commanding officer. You see a man accustomed to undercover work when you watch Iago sounding out Cassio about what a 'dish' Desdemona is.

Othello is a man of honour and gentility who expects the best of people. He is also a man who keeps his own counsel. He is a loner, a solitary stranger. Sometimes he can be oddly secretive: he does *not* tell his friend Brabantio that he is courting Desdemona. He does *not* tell Iago why he has been passed over for lieutenant.

As I have written before, 'Othello does not walk into the world of strangers feeling dependent on their grace; he walks into it expecting them to be dependent on him for wisdom, for knowledge, for experience ... Othello is a superior human being, but not a superman who would exploit others. He possesses grace.'* He sees a compatible grace in Desdemona, and that is one reason he loves her. Grace mates with grace (unity seeking itself). Shakespeare elevates these two characters so that we see that they live on the same plane, as kindred spirits, especially in contrast to the worlds they live in. In her innocence and goodness, Desdemona expects grace of others. Othello, being blessed with grace, demands it of others. When we know that Othello is endowed with grace and that he has been elevated by his culture, we are better equipped to comprehend the drama in the fall – a fall from great heights, from paradise into chaos. This is a fall that Iago has already experienced, when he is passed over for the promotion he wants.

After all the battles and the hardship and the glory, Othello is ready for another chapter of his life. All the adventures that he related to Desdemona's father, and that she overheard, lead her to say, 'If you know someone who loves me, you tell him how to tell that story, and you've got me.' That story ends with her, and the new story begins with her.

So the production of this play needs to dramatize more

---

* James Earl Jones and Penelope Niven, *Voices and Silences* (New York: Scribner, 1993; Simon & Schuster, 1994; Proscenium/Limelight Edition, 2002), 157.

than Othello the warrior. We need to see the peaceful, married Othello. I don't know whether Othello would be happy if he never fought another military campaign, but I know he would not be happy if he did not have Desdemona in his life. He is able to reflect on it in her presence after he's trapped in the confusion about whether she has been unfaithful. He says,

> Had it pleas'd heaven
> To try me with affliction, had he rain'd
> All kinds of sores and shames on my bare head,
> Steep'd me in poverty to the very lips,
> Given to captivity me and my hopes,
> I should have found in some part of my soul
> A drop of patience; but, alas, to make me
> The fixed figure, for the time of scorn
> To point his slow unmoving fingers at . . . oh, oh.
> Yet could I bear that too, well, very well:
> But there, where I have garner'd up my heart,
> Where either I must live or bear no life,
> The fountain, from the which my current runs,
> Or else dries up, to be discarded thence,
> Or keep it as a cistern, for foul toads
> To knot and gender in! Turn thy complexion there;
> Patience, thy young and rose-lipp'd cherubin;
> I here look grim as hell!
> (Act IV, scene ii)

Othello is saying that he can bear almost anything except a threat to his marriage, a corruption of his mate – 'the fountain, from the which my current runs, / Or else dries up'. I take 'current' to mean 'progeny'. This can mean only one thing to me: Othello is hoping that the new chapter of his life will not be just about the loving husband, but about the man who is ready to recycle himself with his wife.

15

We can't deal with the issue of children and fertility without dealing with the question of Othello's potency and sexuality. The issue of Othello's sex life has probably preoccupied more people than the question of Othello's colour. Unfortunately, there are even instances when this play has been taken too personally by racist observers who liked to think of Othello as a neutered black male, a eunuch; but most of the debate about whether Othello is a sexually complete man focuses on his rationale for taking Desdemona with him to Cyprus. He says to the Duke and the Senate,

> I therefore beg it not
> To please the palate of my appetite,
> Nor to comply with heat, the young affects
> In my defunct, and proper satisfaction,
> But to be free and bounteous of her mind;
> And heaven defend your good souls that you think
> I will your serious and great business scant
> For she is with me; . . . no, when light-wing'd toys
> And feather'd Cupid, foils with wanton dullness
> My speculative and active instruments,
> That my disports corrupt and taint my business,
> Let housewives make a skillet of my helm,
> And all indign and base adversities
> Make head against my reputation.
>
> (Act I, scene iii)

The variorum edition of *Othello* gives us a footnote nearly four pages long about the lively debate over the meaning of the words Shakespeare puts in Othello's mouth here.[*] For centuries, it has been asked, 'What do you mean, "defunct"? Did

[*] Horace Howard Furness, editor, *Othello: The New Variorum Edition* (Philadelphia: J. B. Lippincott & Company, 1886; Mineola, New York: Dover Edition, 2000), 72–6.

some early scrivener make a mistake? Did Shakespeare instead actually write "Distinct" or "Disjunct" or "Defenc't" or "Default"?' There are editors of Shakespeare's texts who have concluded that the passage is corrupt (not part of the original text).* But great store has been set by this passage, which has been interpreted to mean that Othello and Desdemona have no sexual relationship because Othello is older and impotent. That also contributes to Othello's uneasiness about satisfying his wife: if he can't, others must be doing it.

On the contrary, I think Othello is simply saying, 'My youth ain't what it used to be.' After all, Othello himself later tells us 'for I am declin'd / Into the vale of years, – yet that's not much . . .' (Act III, scene iii). In other words, he is saying that he is not *that* old.

Othello talks to the Duke about his desire to take his bride with him to Cyprus. After all, her father has declined to let her stay with him while her husband goes to war: when the Duke has suggested that she stay with her father, Brabantio responds, 'I'll not have it so.' 'Nor I,' Othello echoes; and Desdemona says, 'Nor I, I would not there reside, / To put my father in impatient thoughts / By being in his eye' (Act I, scene iii). Othello anticipates that the Senate will have two concerns about Desdemona's presence in Cyprus: that he is just indulging himself physically, and that he will be so busy 'disporting' (or engaging in sexual 'sports') with Desdemona that he won't keep his mind on his job, which is to win the war against the Turks. He is assuring the Venetian Senate that he needs his wife for more than sex, and that no matter how much 'disporting' goes on, his work will not suffer.

Then, at the end of that scene, Othello leads his wife away for what may be interpreted as sexual intimacy, saying,

* See, for instance, Honigmann, note 265, 152.

Come, Desdemona, I have but an hour
Of love, of worldly matters, and direction,
To spend with thee; we must obey the time.

The themes of love and the issues of marriage can be taken
personally (and, yes, even too personally). Othello is not lying
when he says about Brabantio, his wife's father, 'Her father
lov'd me.' He is not deluding himself. Why not take the word
for its face value? There has been genuine love between those
two strong men – Othello the Moorish general and Brabantio
the Venetian senator. Othello has been a beloved guest in the
house of Brabantio. Of course, this relationship was established before Desdemona and Othello were married. For
Brabantio, it disintegrates immediately once Othello becomes
the older man 'seducing' his young daughter, and doing so
behind his back, with no regard for the conventions of
courtship and marriage.

Modern interpreters may try to impose something Freudian
on the Othello–Desdemona age difference, but I reject that
notion. It trivializes the meaning that Shakespeare invested in
the word 'love'. It makes the idea of love petty. Shakespeare
wrote about passion, not about mere emotion. The feelings
expressed in this play always transcend emotions, and they are
more universal.

On Shakespeare's stage, love, when it is a passion, surpasses
anything Freudian or sexual. It leaves room for the ultimate
love that Jesus spoke of. I don't mean just platonic love, but
passionate love. And that's the only kind of love that works in
Othello.

Ethnicity and Culture in Othello

> I saw Othello's visage in his mind . . .
>
> Desdemona to the Duke (Act I, scene iii)

Shakespeare is writing about love and relationships, trust and jealousy, truth and illusion, peace and war, unity and chaos, good and evil, paradise and hell. Themes of love – romantic, platonic or otherwise – have often provoked a consideration of the issues of ethnicity and culture in *Othello*. Ashley Montagu has written that race is a concept concocted for a very particular reason and purpose, and 'has no basis in scientific fact or any other kind of demonstrable fact', but is 'compounded of impure wishful thinking' and 'muddied myth'.* Montagu pointed out that the 'hereditary or biological conception of race differences' developed 'as a direct result of the trade in slaves by European merchants'.† Race was a convenient category to put people in, especially when it could be manipulated to keep the Western mind feeling superior; but institutional racism as we know it did not exist in Shakespeare's time.

When applied to skin colour, the word 'black' in Shakespeare's day usually referred to people whose skin might be darker than that of the typical Caucasian. In *A Midsummer Night's Dream* (Act III, scene ii), a play where there is no ethnic stress, Lysander says with disdain to Hermia, who is a brunette, 'Away, you Ethiope!' When Othello refers to himself as black, as in: 'Haply, for I am black . . .' (Act III, scene iii), it is a

---

* Ashley Montagu, *Man's Most Dangerous Myth: The Fallacy of Race* (Cleveland and New York: The World Publishing Company, 1969), 34.
† Montagu, 38.

'What if?' remark – more curiosity than worry about colour differences. A Westernized black man's life depends on his deference to colour. Othello's life does not depend on his deference to the concept of colour.

Paul Robeson observed that the Renaissance, for all its glories, and the voyages of discovery opened a Pandora's box because of the resulting expansion of national consciousness. Montagu wrote that the eighteenth-century voyages of discovery 'opened up to the view of Europe many new varieties of mankind – people hitherto undreamed of . . . Soon inhabitants of the most distant parts of the world began to be described, pictured . . .'* This led to colour awareness, racism, and the pseudo-scientific categorization of race. The concept of race was invented for scientific and economic convenience.

Prior to this time, however, the concept did not exist, even during times of widespread slavery. 'Scientific' categories were established to classify human beings, animals and other creatures previously unknown. In the Elizabethan chain of being, the king took precedence over the peasant; the lion took precedence over the dog; the oak took precedence over the elm tree. It was later, with the new concept of race, that the white European took precedence over the Moor or the 'Ethiope'.

Shakespeare created three characters who were Moors: the Prince of Morocco in *The Merchant of Venice*; Aaron the Moor in *Titus Andronicus*; and Othello. By the fifteenth century Europeans often referred to Africans as Moors, whether they were the lighter-skinned Moroccans or Mauretanians of northern Africa, or the darker-skinned people of other regions of the continent.

When Portuguese mariners exploring the coasts of West Africa began bringing African slaves to Europe, the term 'black-

* Montagu, 47.

amoor' came into use. Of Shakespeare's three Moors, Aaron is known as a blackamoor, Othello is referred to as 'a noble Moor', and the Prince of Morocco is described as a 'tawny Moor'. The Prince of Morocco is pure fun. 'Mislike me not for my complexion,' he says to Portia, the beautiful Venetian lady he is courting, and then he goes on in detail about how he got to be so black and beautiful. Aaron the Moor is pure villain, a black Iago with less to say and even more lives to wreck. Yet these two are much more readily understood than Othello, who was, I like to think, a mystery even to Shakespeare.

The Elizabethan audience associated 'blackness' with evil and death; therefore they were not surprised to see wicked Aaron the Moor wreaking havoc in a play. The Prince of Morocco is something of a fool for love, but at least – to the relief of many, including the outspoken seventeenth-century critic Thomas Rymer – he did not wind up with the girl.

But Othello – what a perplexing protagonist he must have seemed to Shakespeare's fans. Othello is a noble and cultured stranger from a foreign land. He wins the heart of the fairest damsel in Venice. He was controversial from the beginning, and he still is. Shakespeare could have found a prototype of the noble Moor in the Moorish ambassador to Queen Elizabeth in 1600. A seventeenth-century artist painted a surviving portrait of that ambassador.[*]

Since the seventeenth century some commentators on the plays, such as Thomas Rymer, have suffered from a disease (a 'dis-ease') that would later be defined as racism. Rymer (1641–1713) was an archaeologist as well as an author, and is best known for his attack on Shakespeare's plays, particularly the tragedies, in *A Short View of Tragedy* in 1693. Rymer and others have speculated about the significance of Othello's

---

[*] See, for instance, Honigmann, 2 and 29–31.

ethnicity and of the Moorish general's marriage to the Venetian maiden. E. A. J. Honigmann notes that Rymer deemed the moral of *Othello* to be 'a caution to all Maidens of Quality how, without their Parents consent, they run away with Blackamoors'.[*] Rymer couldn't handle the idea that Othello could have been a sub-Saharan African man – a black man. Rymer said *in essence*, 'Oh, Othello must be Semitic. He must be an Arab with long, straight hair. Othello's hair can't be "woolly".' Rymer implies this in spite of the specific references in the text of the play, such as Roderigo's reference to Othello as 'the thicklips' (Act I, scene i). Said Rymer, 'Should the Poet have provided such a Husband for an only daughter of any noble Peer in *England*, the Black-amoor must have chang'd his Skin, to look our House of Lords in the face.'[†]

Iago manipulates responses to Othello's ethnicity throughout the play. What's very interesting is that racial bias does not seem to exist in *Othello* until it is created by Iago. In the very beginning, Iago approaches every character in his or her unbiased state, including Desdemona's father. Although he loves Othello, Brabantio has no idea that there is an alliance between his daughter and this foreign general who has been a welcome and beloved guest in his house. The father's job is to guard his daughter. Desdemona has committed a 'treason of the blood', Brabantio says (Act I, scene i): she and Othello have not sought his permission to marry. For him, this behaviour violates the fundamental order of family life. It is a dis-unity. Desdemona and Othello have fractured a code or a custom. For Brabantio, when they do not seek his consent, the situation moves from

[*] Thomas Rymer, *The Tragedies of the Last Age, consider'd and examin'd [with] A Short View of Tragedy; its original, excellency, and corruption. With some reflections on Shakspear, and other practitioners for the stage.* (London: Richard Baldwin, 1692–3), quoted in Honigmann, 29.
[†] Rymer, 101, quoted in Furness, op. cit., 51.

being uncustomary to being unnatural, and that leads his mind to accept other ideas of how unnatural it is.

Iago chooses a contentious, provocative way of revealing this alliance to Brabantio: he suggests there has been a kidnapping, perhaps even a rape. Rather than telling Brabantio the truth, Iago colours the story to evoke shock and fear. I've always believed that he creates racism where none existed in Brabantio. That pattern follows through the whole story. One by one, Iago poisons everybody. It's as if he wants to infect the entire society with the 'dis-ease' of racism.

In the first scene of Act I, Roderigo calls Othello 'the thick-lips'. Roderigo's use of this word triggers a sharp response from Iago. On the heels of that, Iago has a plan, hatching out of the thin air of Roderigo's breath. He urges Roderigo to join him in rousing Brabantio and putting in the worst possible light the news that his daughter has married Othello. They will 'poison' Brabantio's delight in his daughter; they will 'incense' Desdemona's relatives; they will 'plague' Brabantio 'with flies'. Then the insults pour from Iago's mouth as if he himself is newly infected: Othello is a thief, 'an old black ram' who is 'tupping' Brabantio's 'white ewe'. Othello is a 'devil' who 'will make a grandsire' of Brabantio. He is a 'Barbary horse,' a 'lascivious Moor', 'making the beast with two backs' with Desdemona. Othello is 'an extravagant and wheeling stranger' (a wandering, free-wheeling foreigner) who has made off with Desdemona.

Brabantio is a mature man, jolted from his sleep and confronted with shocking news about his only child. He is a human being responding to a panic of ideas. Soon he, too, is verbally attacking his friend Othello as a 'foul thief', a wizard who has surely enchained Desdemona with magic spells or 'abused her delicate youth with drugs or minerals'. Otherwise, Brabantio wants to know, why would his 'tender, fair and happy' daughter suddenly 'Run from her guardage to the sooty bosom / Of such a thing' as Othello? (Act I, scene ii).

Such is the fever that the disease of racism generates in Brabantio. He tries to infect the Senate with his outrage, telling them, 'For if such actions may have passage free / Bond-slaves, and pagans, shall our statesmen be.' Brabantio has loved Othello, but Brabantio is now inflamed over the permission issue. How could this marriage have come about without his knowledge and approval? For Brabantio, Desdemona and Othello's greatest offence is their failure to seek his permission for their marriage. His duty and right as a father is to protect his daughter until the transition is made to a legitimate husband. His last act of 'guardage' should have been to give consent for the marriage. He has been denied this proper step in the right order of his life. Brabantio can only see this as a violent offence.

Historically, as actors and directors have wrestled with production questions, they have experimented with various depictions of Othello's ethnicity and culture. For instance, I understand that Sir Laurence Olivier patterned his Othello after a friend, a black man from the Caribbean. Curiously, the Jamaicans have a different cultural view of race from African-Americans – a less deferential view. However, neither of these views reflects the perspective of the seventeenth-century Moor of Africa, or the seventeenth-century Venetian or Englishman. We are not talking about the 'racism' informed by the American South. This racism presents an inescapable duality that must be considered: as Abraham Lincoln expressed it, 'As I would not be a slave, so I would not be a master.'

I observed in Errol John's 1964 performance of Othello that he was so defensive it was as if he was unconsciously aware of second-class-ness, and this made him guarded. I think that is what Othello is *not*. That guardedness is one of the problems with the stigma of the second-class citizen. It keeps him on edge.

It's why black people have higher blood pressure in the United States. You can even try to use it as a culturally positive thing, but you are still on edge about it, whether you are looking at it positively or negatively. The fact is that you are different; you are separate. Ethnocentrism is a dangerous thing: it keeps you on edge. We don't want an Othello who is on edge about his colour.

Racism involves both the person who dislikes someone because of ethnicity, *and* the person who is the victim of that dislike. In Shakespeare's *The Merchant of Venice* (Act I, scene iii) the characters' dislike of Shylock is very clear, and he reciprocates. Shylock says of Antonio, 'I hate him for he is a Christian.' Iago says, 'I hate the Moor.' Iago and Shylock evoke an almost identical credo of hatred. Ironically, with Shylock it is the victim of prejudice rather than the perpetrator who expresses the animosity.

In *Titus Andronicus* Aaron the Moor is accepted as the queen's paramour. No one makes note of his being black; it is not an issue. In a film version of this play in 2000, director and adaptor Julie Taymor realized that racism becomes important only when it is used as a tactic to demonize the character of Aaron – as if he were not demon enough already – and to defeat him. It is a child who suggests that a good reason to kill a fly is that it is a 'black fly'.

Iago, too, sets in motion this demonizing process, creating racism on the spot, improvising as he goes. If it is true, as Othello says, that Brabantio loves him, how can Brabantio all of a sudden dislike black people? How did this happen? These days, we would call Iago's devious strategy 'disinformation'. Iago is improvising but he is quite good at it. That's his job. The first scene of *Othello* is about disinformation. Iago takes part of what is true and distorts it, and the infectious disease begins to take hold.

The Tragedy of Iago

> Were I the Moor, I would not be Iago:
> In following him, I follow but myself. . . .
> For when my outward action does demonstrate
> The native act, and figure of my heart,
> In complement extern, 'tis not long after,
> But I will wear my heart upon my sleeve,
> For doves to peck at: I am not what I am.
>
> Iago to Roderigo (Act I, scene i)

I contend that Iago is the most complex character that Shakespeare ever created. He has also been called vengeful and nihilistic, a man of 'diseased intellectual activity, with an almost perfect indifference to moral good or evil'.[*] Harold Goddard has described Iago as 'perhaps the most terrific indictment of pure intellect in the literature of the world'.[†] Iago is dangerous to those who love and trust him because he has convinced them over time that he loves them in return, and that he can be trusted absolutely.

Early on, Iago seems to become the stage manager of the play. Actually, he sets events in motion and lucks out: everything falls into his lap. The resulting intrigue and duplicity give rise to the tragedy; but Iago is not in control of events: he does not have everything in the bag.

---

[*] William Hazlitt, quoted in Harold Bloom, *Shakespeare: The Invention of the Human* (New York: Riverhead Books, 1998), 433. See Harold Bloom on Iago's nihilism and his 'sublimely negative' genius (433–9).
[†] Harold C. Goddard, *The Meaning of Shakespeare* (Chicago and London: The University of Chicago Press, 1951), vol. II, 76.

Iago is a man who is used to scamming his way out of trouble. It's not that he has laid out a complicated and sinister plan. It just hits him. He improvises. He has, most likely, got Othello out of trouble before, too, on the battlefield and in Venetian society. Iago seems so cool in the presence of others, but we should see the other side of cool: there, Iago is not the Machiavellian figure, the slick devil pulling all the puppet strings. Despite his cocky promise to Roderigo that 'There are many events in the womb of time, which will be delivered' (Act I, scene iii), I think Iago is more desperate than is usually recognized.

In his *Shakespeare: The Invention of the Human* (1998) Harold Bloom observes that we don't meet the heroic characters such as Othello and Cassio until Iago has got a running start, so we as actors and audience have to be alert to how the other characters are accounted for in the play. It is also interesting to see how the other characters account for Iago. Othello, for instance, says

> This fellow's of exceeding honesty,
> And knows all qualities, with a learned spirit,
> Of human dealing . . .
> (Act III, scene iii)

Ironically, Othello is wrong about Iago's honesty, but has always been right about Iago's savvy about 'qualities . . . / Of human dealing', or human psychology. Iago knows what makes people tick and he manipulates that knowledge with devastating results.

The tragedies that happen to Othello and Desdemona are grand, classical tragedies. As they consider the grandeur of these tragedies, directors might profit by looking at the size of Verdi's opera, *Otello*. There is a much more modern tragedy in the character of Iago. His is a very contemporary tragedy that should not be thrown away. To view Iago as a jokester and a clown – just a Machiavellian gangster – is to demean and distort the characters of Iago *and* Othello, as well as to diminish the tragedy of the whole play and that of the character of Iago; but it takes a strong director and a strong vision of the play to lead the actor playing Iago into the tragic and mysterious depths of Iago's true nature. The easy way is to make the jokes and to be the gamesman. It should never be easy for this gamesman, and Iago himself observes how complex it is: '. . . 'tis here, but yet confused; / Knavery's plain face is never seen, till us'd' (Act II, scene i).

I am looking for a model for Iago. To understand him, I am still looking everywhere except where Machiavelli trod, or where Rymer poisoned. We have to understand Iago's fall from grace. So who is a role model? Darth Vader?

Consider Lucifer, who fell because he failed to 'play the game' with God. Consider Cordelia who was banished for not 'playing the game' with Lear. Iago feels that he has lost to Cassio, who plays the game better. He certainly works for a boss who is so solitary and secretive as not to assure Iago of his real value. This causes Iago anguish, as he tells us at the outset of the play, when he is denied the office of lieutenant to Othello: '. . . by the faith of man, / I know my price, I am worth no worse a place (Act I, scene i). And Iago's real value comes from his sinister side. He is the Goebbels to Hitler, the Beria to Stalin. Othello, while no Hitler or Stalin, was secretive and solitary, and he did not get the word out to people very well. He could have had a discussion with Iago about the appointment; he could have had a discussion with Brabantio about the marriage. Othello's failure to do so contributes mightily to the estrangement of Brabantio, his beloved friend, and to the animosity of Iago, his trusted ensign.

In his *Asimov's Guide to Shakespeare* (1970), Isaac Asimov

refs to the opening scene of the play as being about one
character – Roderigo – being double-crossed.* Roderigo is
paying Iago a lot of money to intercede for him with
Desdemona. Somehow Iago has convinced Roderigo that he
has power and influence, but he has come up short.
Desdemona has married Othello. Roderigo is incensed.
Roderigo is not just a dupe. Rather than being a gullible pup,
Roderigo can be very dangerous to Iago. Roderigo is about
the power of money. He is not happy with Iago when he
learns of Desdemona's marriage. In the very first lines of the
play, Roderigo says to Iago,

> Tush, never tell me, I take it much unkindly
> That thou, Iago, who hast had my purse
> As if the strings were thine, shouldst know of this.
>
> (Act I, scene i)

This scene is bad news, and now Iago is in trouble. It is
important to reveal that. Roderigo happens to be the first person Iago deceives and infects. Duping is small potatoes, but
this is infection, which is not small potatoes. It is interesting
to note how many times Iago himself uses the vocabulary of
poison, infection and disease. He even applies these images to
himself – for instance, as he speculates about Othello's possible seduction of Emilia. The thought, he says, 'Doth like a
poisonous mineral gnaw my inwards . . .' (Act II, scene i). And
during Othello's trance, Iago says, 'Work on, / My medicine,
work' (Act IV, scene i).

Iago has to get very busy talking his way out of trouble,
and in that talk he tries everything: he slanders everyone; he
blames everyone but himself. That is an example of how

---

* Isaac Asimov, *Asimov's Guide to Shakespeare* (New York: Wings Books,
1970), vol. I, 611.

desperate he is, and how he operates in an almost chronic state of desperation.

The Iago–Roderigo relationship is complex. The theme of money keeps cropping up between the two characters. Iago is now convinced that money is, for him, the only pathway to power, and he has latched on to Roderigo and Roderigo's purse. In fact, some of Iago's greatest lines are about money. When Roderigo learns that Desdemona is married, he tells Iago he will drown himself because he cannot live without her. After Iago talks him out of that dire threat, Roderigo says, 'I am chang'd,' and in the Folio version adds: 'I'll sell all my land' (Act I, scene iii).

It is a temptation to try to get a laugh from that line, but it's actually a warning: Roderigo is reminding Iago that, for him, seducing Desdemona is serious business. He'll risk all his wealth for it, and he is depending on Iago, as well as paying him, to make it happen.

The key factor of money establishes not only the relationship between Roderigo and Iago, but Iago's relation to the whole play. He is a common man who lacks the social wherewithal that Othello, Desdemona, Cassio and even Roderigo possess. He occupies a rung further down the social ladder, and where he is, he is not going to be successful. He was counting on being elevated to Othello's lieutenant. Was this delusion? Casting is important here: Iago has to appear to qualify as the general's lieutenant, at least on the battlefield, even if he lacks Cassio's social finesse, and, like Lucifer, he should be gorgeous to look at. The reason for his fall is enigmatic to him. He was not passed over because he lacked social appeal. He lacks the formal social graces of a higher station, but he is very personable and very smart.

When Iago perceives that he has been crossed, he becomes quite dangerous to the whole society and he will take it all down with him. Now everything tastes like shit in his mouth, including his own marriage. He has not found a Desdemona to fulfil his life. He believes his station, his wealth, his chance at having a life – all have been ruined when Othello has passed over him for promotion.

Having inflamed Brabantio with a misrepresentation of what has happened between Desdemona and Othello, Iago more subtly tries to inflame Othello by telling him that Brabantio

> . . . prated,
> And spoke such scurvy and provoking terms
> Against your honour,
> That with the little godliness I have
> I did full hard forbear him . . .
>> (Act I, scene ii)

Iago warns that Brabantio is 'much belov'd' and powerful:

> . . . he will divorce you,
> Or put upon you what restraint, and grievance,
> That law (with all his might to enforce it on)
> Will give him cable.

Othello is almost aware that Iago is overreacting. Iago has to be very careful because of that. He has to be very convincing. He has to put on a mask of concerned sincerity.

Iago is sharp-witted, and often glibly tosses off statements that can mean more or less than they seem to mean. We see examples of his gift for the play-by-play in the scene on the quay at Cyprus, where he and Desdemona and others are waiting for news of Othello's life or death. Until the governor arrives, Desdemona is the governor. She has a responsibility to the others until her husband arrives, and she exercises her authority. In effect, she says to Iago, 'Let you entertain us.' She asks him, in essence, to entertain the troops by giving a sort of USO (United Services Organization) skit. In the colourful, even bawdy dialogue that follows, Iago is not merely taking advantage of women and weak soldiers; he is following the order he has been given to let loose his wit.

Iago's brain is probably as rich as Hamlet's, if not richer. That makes Iago's life even more tragic. Such a mind is a terrible thing to waste, and it doesn't have a shot in the world. Iago evokes Janus – the two-faced god (Act I, scene ii). He says to Roderigo, 'Were I the Moor, I would not be Iago . . . I am not what I am' (Act I, scene i). E. A. J. Honigmann, among others, points out that this line is a contrast to God's statement to Moses: 'I am that I am,' in Exodus 3:14; and to St Paul's 'By the grace of God I am what I am,' in First Corinthians 15:10. *

But when Iago says, 'I am not what I am,' he seems to me full of regret, as if to suggest, 'The "I am" is what I could have been and should have been.' There is a universal complaint here: I am nobody. I know I have a soul; but nothing else confirms that. I am not what I am.

Consider him as a Janus figure. Each of Iago's Janus 'faces' is genuine; they just look out in opposite directions, as the faces of Janus do. When Iago is with those he loves, he loves them. When he is not, we have a quite different Iago. Whatever this is, it is complete. If it is schizophrenia, it's profound schizophrenia. Iago is able to manipulate it within himself. When he says to Othello, 'You know I love you,' he *does* love Othello, believe it or not. As much as Iago says to Roderigo, 'I hate the Moor,' he loves him. I don't mean homosexually, either, but soul to soul. Othello and Iago have shared a military life together; they have built that trust between them. Ironically, Iago has a great deal of fear-based respect for Othello, yet he tries to convince Roderigo that he hates the Moor.

* See Honigmann, 120, note 64.

None of the other characters in the play would suspect that Iago does not love them, too, including Cassio and Desdemona. At first, Roderigo, supposedly gullible, is the only one to suspect that there is less than love going on; but at some point, prior to the drunkenness in Act II, scene iii, Cassio becomes very suspicious of Iago. If it were not for Cassio's weakness for alcohol, he probably would have resolved the problem that day; but he gets drunk and he loses focus. Iago sets up the drunken brawl that leads to Cassio's disgrace. Now Cassio is beholden to Iago, and he's sunk.

The wonderful 'temptation' scene between Othello and Iago should work plausibly. This is the pivotal moment in the play, when Iago seeks to sabotage Othello's faith in Desdemona's fidelity and Cassio's honesty. Iago masks his innuendoes with seemingly sympathetic questions aimed at the vulnerable shield of Othello's trust: 'Did Michael Cassio, when you woo'd my lady, / Know of your love?' Iago asks (Act III, scene iii). He feeds Othello with intimations and platitudes: 'Men should be that they seem . . .'

> O, beware jealousy;
> It is the green-eyed monster, which doth mock
> That meat it feeds on.

In the guise of loyalty, love and friendship, Iago offers seemingly well-intentioned advice: 'Look to your wife, observe her well with Cassio.' He warns Othello against the wiles of Venetian women, reminds him that Desdemona deceived her own father by secretly marrying Othello, and speculates about why Desdemona chose Othello over 'many proposed matches / Of her own clime, complexion and degree . . .' As Iago's deftly planted seeds of confusion take hold, Othello demands proof that, as Iago insinuates, Desdemona has betrayed the marriage. It is then that Iago turns to outright deceit – fabricating the story that Cassio has spoken in his dreams of a love affair with Desdemona, and planting Desdemona's handkerchief in Cassio's quarters.

This temptation is driven by the fact that, technically and professionally, Iago is supposed to tell Othello anything Othello wants to know. The more Iago appears to resist sharing information, the more tempting that information seems to Othello, because he believes that Iago is trying to protect him. The temptation works much better if Iago gives the impression that it hurts him even to think about telling Othello what he suspects. It is as if you are watching two people trade an infection between each other. In this case the disease is jealousy, confusion, disintegration. Iago is jealous and Othello is being tempted to jealousy, infected with confusion, to the point that his inner and outer worlds begin to disintegrate. This exchange should happen as gently as diseases are transmitted from one person to another – not wilfully, not aggressively, but just very quietly and subtly.

The director should help Iago find the pain and the tragedy in this drama, not settle for cheap shots and jokes that reduce the other characters to cannon fodder for the fusillade of Iago's wit: cheap shots dilute the serious themes and the tragic impact of the play. But Iago was born with this wit. What does he do with it? He does not have Hamlet's station in life. A contrast with Hamlet is fitting because Iago has Hamlet's wit, but he learns Richard III's will.

As I have said before, Iago is the equivalent of a modern undercover agent. He has to be credible. Clever as Iago is, he can never afford to play Roderigo easy. He tries to re-ignite Roderigo's passion for Desdemona, and he promises that he will help him win her – no matter that she is the 'super-subtle Venetian' now married to the 'erring Barbarian'. Never mind that, once the Moor and Desdemona are married, it would be illegal to 'cuckold' Othello and seduce his wife. Iago has to hatch a plot to keep money coming in from Roderigo.

He will take Roderigo to Cyprus. There, Iago will 'cuckold' Roderigo, Cassio and Othello – all three – in a scheme that, if successful, will bring Iago Roderigo's money, Cassio's position and Othello's fall, and Roderigo Desdemona's body. Iago lays out his purpose and his justification in a soliloquy:

> . . . I hate the Moor,
> And it is thought abroad that 'twixt my sheets
> He's done my office. I know not if't be true . . .
> Yet I, for mere suspicion in that kind,
> Will do, as if for surety: he holds me well,
> The better shall my purpose work on him.
> Cassio's a proper man, let me see now,
> To get this place, and to make up my will,
> A double knavery . . . how, how? . . . let me see,
> After some time, to abuse Othello's ear,
> That he is too familiar with his wife:
> He has a person and a smooth dispose,
> To be suspected, fram'd to make women false:
> The Moor a free and open nature too,
> That thinks men honest that but seems to be so:
> And will as tenderly be led by the nose . . .
> As asses are.
> I have't, it is engender'd; Hell and night
> Must bring this monstrous birth to the world's light.
>
> (Act I, scene iii)

There is Iago's desperate plan in a nutshell, and his uncertainty. He has 'engender'd' events, but he recognizes that he does not have the power to 'birth' them: 'Hell and night' must do that work. As he has said, ''Tis here, but yet confus'd . . .' In other words, Iago's plan is not all laid out, and the result is not a foregone conclusion. He plants Desdemona's handkerchief. He gives evidence that can't be contested; he is fully aware of that. He is improvising, right to the end of the play: 'This is the night / That either makes me, or fordoes me quite' (Act V, scene i).

Othello's last speech asks that, in reporting his actions, witnesses should

> Speak of them as they are; nothing extenuate,
> Nor set down aught in malice; then must you speak
> Of one that lov'd not wisely, but too well:
> Of one not easily jealous, but being wrought,
> Perplex'd in the extreme; of one whose hand,
> Like the base Indian, threw a pearl away,
> Richer than all his tribe . . .
>   (Act V, scene ii)

For a director to let Iago play for farce is to throw away pearls of great price. At the beginning of Act III, scene i, the Clown enters. There is one clown in this play, and the play does not ask Iago to be another clown. We need to see Iago as a human being. Ultimately, this makes his tragedy all the more terrifying.

The Tragedy of Desdemona

> Excellent wretch, perdition catch my soul,
> But I do love thee! and when I love thee not,
> Chaos is come again.
>
> Othello speaking to Desdemona (Act III, scene iii)

Who was Desdemona and what was she to Othello? What are the keys that give us insight into what she was to him before he begins to doubt himself? You have to start with Desdemona's name. She is a counterbalance to Iago, who is ultimately assessed to be a demon. She is the 'dis-demon', the good angel to Iago's Lucifer. That gives us a symbolic definition of who and what she is. Desdemona possesses grace, beauty, virtue, intelligence, fairness – qualities that attracted Othello. She seems to find the best nature in every person she deals with, especially with Othello, even in his worst state.

Their love story begins simply enough: he relates the saga of his life, and she falls in love with him. The love affair between Othello and Desdemona happens in secrecy, under cover. (It might be argued that Iago is not the only undercover agent in this play.) That is why it explodes in such a horrible way for her father. Brabantio is the classic protective father, very particular about his daughter's suitors, and he rightfully owes her his 'guardage', his protection. He rejects Roderigo when he tries to court Desdemona. Brabantio was not even asked to consider Othello as a suitor.

Desdemona's elopement is a woman's act of resolution. She has often been dismissed as a wilful girl; but there is something much stronger than wilfulness in her. She was born into privilege, and accustomed to it, so that she would think nothing of using her privilege; yet she is not simply petulant or wilful. She is wilful and more – as Princess Diana was in our own time. Near the end of her life, Princess Diana's choice of lover was heedless of culture. She was reaching for a larger cause. She believed she had a larger mission, a larger calling. She began to prove it as she championed causes and charities. We all accepted that about her; otherwise we would not have mourned her death as we did worldwide.

Desdemona perceives a wider world and a larger cause. Her marriage to Othello is not an act of rebellion, but an act of conviction. She does not violate her father here; Desdemona's first allegiance is to her husband. At best, she tries to broaden the cosmos to include Othello, who comes to her from another world. This is her nature. I believe it is important to take all this into account as we look for the richest possible interpretation for all the characters, especially Desdemona.

She tells the Duke:

> I saw Othello's visage in his mind,
> And to his honours, and his valiant parts
> Did I my soul and fortunes consecrate . . .
>   (Act I, scene iii)

She has chosen Othello as much for his mind and spirit as for his physical presence. She has found the courage to challenge her father and convention to marry this man she loves. Just as the marriage takes place in privacy, Othello keeps his feelings for his wife very private. Whereas other Shakespearean characters speak publicly of their wives in superlatives and serenades, Othello keeps his own counsel about his love for Desdemona. Given the Moorish tradition of art, poetry and song, you wonder why Othello doesn't offer songs and poems for his beloved Desdemona. He is, after all, a gentle soul, despite his lifelong experience as a warrior. The closest he comes to uttering a song about her comes when they meet at Cyprus. Something lyrical happens between them. Othello says,

> It gives me wonder great as my content
> To see you here before me: O my soul's joy,
> If after every tempest come such calmness,
> May the winds blow, till they have waken'd death,
> And let the labouring bark climb hills of seas,
> Olympus-high, and duck again as low
> As hell's from heaven. If it were now to die
> 'Twere now to be most happy, for I fear
> My soul hath her content so absolute,
> That not another comfort, like to this
> Succeeds in unknown fate.
>
> (Act II, scene i)

This odd tribute to her proclaims that their love has survived war and storm. Ironically, it also foreshadows Othello's fate. He will, in fact, never again know a time of such complete comfort and content as he experiences in this moment that is 'too much of joy'.

Desdemona's response is a sort of prayer and prophesy:

> The heavens forbid
> But that our loves and comforts should increase,
> Even as our days do grow.

Othello is saying that he could die at this moment and be happy; but when Desdemona replies, her use of the word 'increase' evokes for me once more the possibility that she and Othello want to have children. Consider the possibility that she could already be pregnant.

In Venice, Othello wants time alone with his wife:

Come, Desdemona, I have but an hour
Of love, of worldly matters, and direction,
To spend with thee . . .
(Act I, scene iii)

From the outset, it is clear that this is going to be an exciting relationship where neither person is going to be moulded
to the other person. It is going to be individualistic, unique.
Whatever the customs of her time and place, Desdemona is
out to redefine them in terms of grace, cultural elevation, civic
responsibility – all the fine qualities she sees in Othello. She is
even willing to wear the trappings of the soldier. Portia does
this in disguise, taking on the trappings of a male lawyer in
The Merchant of Venice. In contrast, Ophelia never goes
beyond being anything but a submissive victim, dressed at the
end in flowers. In extending her rights as a woman, Lady
Macbeth goes too far, as does Tamora in *Titus Andronicus*; but
they have royal status and power to indulge in. There is nothing about royalty or even money in Desdemona's quest. That
is not her concern.

Desdemona is much more than the obedient daughter.
Before she loved Othello she had no reason to show her
colours, to be herself; but she is empowered by love to assert
herself as a person. In so doing, Desdemona redefines
woman's role and the relationship between husband and wife.
She wants to be a fit companion to this man she loves:

I saw Othello's visage in his mind,
And to his honours, and his valiant parts
Did I my soul and fortunes consecrate . . .
(Act I, scene iii)

The Othello Desdemona recognized was an elevated human
being, an extraordinary man, larger than life.

40

We need to pay attention to how Desdemona is described by others. Her father, for instance, emphasizes her extreme innocence. Brabantio calls her

> A maiden never bold of spirit,
> So still and quiet, that her motion
> Blush'd at herself . . .
>> (Act I, scene iii)

Because of his own sense of the world order, Brabantio cannot imagine how his innocent daughter could be captivated by a man so very different in nature, age, country, reputation and 'everything'. He has even said to Roderigo, whom he has earlier forbidden to court Desdemona, 'O that you had had her!' (Act I, scene i).

For Othello, the most telling thing about Desdemona is how she responded to the story of his life. She listened raptly and compassionately. She told Othello she 'wish'd / That heaven had made her such a man'. She never meant, however, that she wanted to be a man. Rather, she hoped that such a man would be made *for* her. Then she thanked Othello and urged him, if he had a friend who loved her, to teach that friend how to tell Othello's story. That would woo her, Desdemona said, and Othello acted on that 'hint', that apparently innocent invitation. He courted her, and, as he told the Senate, 'She loved me for the dangers I had pass'd, / And I lov'd her that she did pity them' (Act I, scene iii).

The question then becomes: was Desdemona infatuated with the adventurous life itself – or with the man who had survived the adventurous life? Most people respect life as an adventure, and for Othello to have had such adventures, and to have wound up on her doorstep, is a marvel to Desdemona. It is irresistible that he has waded through all that life to get to her. She is willing to give a great deal, including her hand in marriage, for that kind of endurance. She is reaching for a larger life than what was carved out for her in Venice.

There is the question of whether Desdemona is a 'rebel' when her father asks her where her obedience lies. She replies,

My noble father,
I do perceive here a divided duty:
To you I am bound for life and education,
My life and education both do learn me
How to respect you; you are lord of all my duty,
I am hitherto your daughter: but here's my husband:
And so much duty as my mother show'd
To you, preferring you before her father,
So much I challenge, that I may profess,
Due to the Moor my lord.

She has assumed a major choice on her own. Was that ordinary? Was that common? If not, this makes a very particular character out of her, although not necessarily a rebellious one. Why not see the richest possible interpretation of Desdemona instead of merely a 'wilful girl'. We need something else, something larger, something that can fulfil the humanity of the play. I think a production is short-changed if the actress playing the part simply evokes a wilful girl. Cassio calls her the 'divine Desdemona'. Harold Goddard wrote that 'one is tempted to assert' that Desdemona 'is the strongest character in all Shakespeare'.* The director Gladys Vaughan believed Desdemona to stand with Othello and Iago as the three strong, central pillars supporting the structure and action of the play.

We can look for warning signs that there may have been delusions in the relationship between Desdemona and Othello, but there are solid declarations of love and desire to

* Goddard, 84.

be together. No matter how obscure some of the poetry is, this is not cold logic, or superficial courtly love; it is heated and passionate. The music of love comes out of Desdemona and Othello even in crisis. I believe Shakespeare's need was to elevate Othello and Desdemona so that we can see that they live on the same plane, as kindred spirits, especially in contrast to the commercial and military worlds they inhabit in Venice.

Yet Desdemona's view of the world transcends Venice. She reckons with a larger, cosmic order. She possesses the courage to choose her own husband, and to defy convention in doing so. Her marriage is important on the level of life and death for her. That is one reason why Othello calls her his 'fair warrior' (Act II, scene i). You see how steadfast she is, even in the face of her own death. She understands the larger order and expects Othello to grasp it as well.

Desdemona has lived a cloistered life, but now she wants to live in the world with Othello. They are aligned in grace in a marriage endowed with grace. Throughout the play, Desdemona has to be strong, but she can't be strong to the detriment of her dignity or her grace. She must be made larger than life, with the soul-size of a heroine. Everything in a production must make Desdemona look as strong a pillar for the play as Othello and Iago. She must be kept centre-focused and in the light.

It is important, too, to remember that, throughout the drama, Desdemona remains steadfastly true to Othello, and to herself. Desdemona takes on total responsibility in her world, and never wavers from it.

The Tragedy of Othello

> The Moor, howbe't that I endure him not,
> Is of a constant, noble, loving nature;
> And I dare think, he'll prove to Desdemona
> A most dear husband . . .
>> Iago, in soliloquy (Act II, scene i)

> . . . nothing extenuate,
> Nor set down aught in malice . . .
>> Othello to Lodovico, Montano, Cassio and Gratiano
>> (Act V, scene ii)

Othello falls from great heights – from paradise to chaos. He kills his wife, and then himself; but I am convinced that it is not jealousy that drives Othello. It is insanity. Othello swings from love and admiration for Desdemona to fury, in the same breath: '. . . a fine woman, a fair woman, a sweet woman!' Othello says. The next moment, he condemns her:

> And let her rot, and perish, and be damned to-night, for she shall not live; no, my heart is turn'd to stone; I strike it, and it hurts my hand: O, the world has not a sweeter creature, she might lie by an emperor's side, and command him tasks.
>> (Act IV, scene i)

Iago interjects, 'Nay, that's not your way,' and Othello responds:

> Hang her, I do but say what she is: so delicate with her needle, an admirable musician, O, she will sing the savageness out of a bear; of so high and plenteous wit and invention!

Not a moment later, Othello swears, 'I will chop her into messes . . . Cuckold me!' and begins to plan to kill her.

How does this come about, and why? Othello has come from a different culture from that of Venice where, by spiritual evolution, he is nobler than anyone else. Desdemona recognizes that in him, and he sees it in her. It is grace. Probably nothing except grace could have brought them together. Othello has been sent into an alien world with this kind of gift, and he goes with benevolence.

The fine life he inherited from Moorish culture left him elevated, especially in the world of soldiers, Iago's world. An elevated person has a great responsibility: to give everyone the benefit of the doubt; to be very judicious. Because he was blessed, Othello owed life more than the average man would owe it. He became extremely blessed with Desdemona as his mate.

Othello is the noble, gallant Moor, the respected general, proven in battle. He has a healthy ego, or he wouldn't be doing what he does, including marrying Desdemona. Othello feels fully qualified to be her suitor and then her husband. He knows that he has performed valuable services for the state, and that these services are appreciated. Like Desdemona, he was born into high station. He tells Iago that he wouldn't relinquish his freedom for all the treasures of the sea if he did not love 'the gentle Desdemona' (Act I, scene ii). This is a key to understanding Othello. His self-assurance is balanced by humility: it has been pointed out that it is ironic that Othello claims to be rude in his speech, then goes on to make one of the most poetic speeches in the whole play. Othello also possesses patience. When he is confronted in the Duke's chambers by an irate Brabantio, in Act I, scene iii, Othello remains calm and composed. Brabantio calls Othello a thief in the wake of his belief that his daughter has been kidnapped and raped. We see Brabantio's hysteria really inflamed, having been stimulated by Iago. Despite the fact that Venice is in the midst of a war emergency, the Duke takes time to hear Brabantio's complaint as he repeats his suspicions about Othello. The Duke then asks Othello for his side of the story.

Again, very calmly and respectfully, Othello acknowledges that he has married Brabantio's daughter. He will be happy to explain how the elopement happened. As he delivers his 'round unvarnish'd tale', Othello responds with a speech that begins with this phrase: 'Her father lov'd me . . .' This is another key phrase, which not only defines Othello's relationship with Brabantio and his family, but also defines Othello. He has been a beloved guest in the house. That's the opposite of being the 'Barbary horse', the 'lascivious Moor', as Iago paints him, and quite the opposite of the exploitative power that Brabantio fears.

As Othello relates the saga of his life, he uses some exotic phrases: '. . . the Cannibals that each other eat, / The Anthropophagi, and men whose heads / Do grow beneath their shoulders' (Act I, scene iii).* In fact, Othello uses such vivid language that some have suggested he is bombastic or delusional. However, as Furness and other writers have noted, Shakespeare most likely put these images in Othello's 'round unvarnish'd tale' because they were part of the accessible literature of his day. Sir Walter Raleigh had written in his *The Discoverie of Guiana*, in 1596, about a nation of people called the Ewaipanoma 'whose heades appeare not above their shoulders' and who were reported to 'have their eyes in their shoulders, and their mouths in the middle of their breasts'.† Such stories were part of the travel lore of the time. In any

---

* See Furness, 56–8, notes, for an interesting discussion of sources Shakespeare may have used as a basis for these references.
† Furness, 56, note 167.

case, I would rather take Othello at his word, just as I want to take all the characters in this play, including Iago, at their word. They are saying either what they know, or what they believe. (This is more difficult, of course, with Iago, for there are times we know he is lying, and if he believes the untruths he speaks, then he verges on paranoia.)

Characteristically, despite the vivid adventures he has to relate, Othello evokes a sense of sureness, a sense of ease and patience. However, even though he is calm and patient in demeanour, he should not be portrayed as always being dispassionate. That may have been a mistake I've made at times when I've approached the role.

As I have emphasized, our aim as actors is to give the broadest, richest interpretation of all the characters. One hopes that the director will feel free to find the simplest interpretation, the one that gives the greatest feel for the character and the content of the play. I'd also like to encourage the director to deal with the new reality that, even though Othello is going to fight a war, his private life has changed profoundly. Now this vital new person – his wife – will share what is to be, as he sees it, perhaps the final chapter of his life.

Othello is going to do battle on Cyprus, and he wants Desdemona to go with him. Even Brabantio accepts this plan, but with a cutting remark: 'So let the Turk of Cyprus us beguile, / We lose it not so long as we can smile . . .' (Act I, scene iii). Now Othello and Desdemona's marriage as an issue has been resolved, except in the minds of Iago and Roderigo.

I have suggested that Roderigo has a dangerous edge, and I must never forget that there can be dangerous edges to Othello, especially when he is with Iago on the streets of Cyprus, quelling the hotheads. Here we see General Othello, righteous and formidable, sternly chastising and disciplining his men for their street brawl:

Are we turn'd Turks, and to ourselves do that
Which heaven has forbid the Ottomites?
For Christian shame, put by this barbarous brawl;
He that stirs next, to carve for his own rage,
Holds his soul light, he dies upon his motion;
Silence that dreadful bell, it frights the isle
From her propriety . . .

(Act II, scene iii)

However controlled he may appear to be, Othello is at white
heat here – not out of control, but lethal; and there is something righteous about him, expressed when he dresses down
the brawlers and dismisses Cassio. He puts a stop to the brawl-
ing, in part out of concern for 'a town of war, / Yet wild, the
people's hearts brim full of fear . . .'

It is quite clear that Cassio is a beloved person to Othello,
though in a different way from Desdemona or Iago; and in the
end, to dismiss Cassio from his rank is stern but righteous.
Desdemona understands the bond between Cassio and
Othello, and in response to Cassio's dismissal she seems to be
saying, 'Oh, come on,' as if she understands the military pro-
tocol. She seems to view this as an act of diplomacy by
Othello, to make an example of Cassio and to appease the
Cypriots. This helps to explain why she feels free to press
Cassio's case with Othello.

Othello has a clear sense of the proper order of things – of
the way the general serves the kingdom; the way his soldiers
comport themselves; the way a husband honours a wife and a
wife honours a husband. This sense of order grows in part out
of his deep sense of honour. He expects the best of everyone.
He especially trusts his ensign and his lieutenant. In a way,
Othello has just taken it for granted that Iago is an honest,
trustworthy man.

Othello also completely trusts his wife – with his life, his heart, his freedom. Unless you make something of that marriage as being Othello's endgame, the rest of it – Othello as a warrior – is not very interesting. In this case, there has to be something to dramatize besides Othello the warrior, or else you end up trying to justify the character as being a warrior, in terms of his life energy. There is no war, because Shakespeare chose for the battle to be resolved by nature, the higher order. A storm wrecked the Turkish fleet. It scattered the Venetians, but they all came back together. The sun comes out; we're home safe. Of all the stories of military heroes in Shakespeare, the issue of the battle and the adversary is almost cursory in this case. In a way, Shakespeare is denying his hero the chance to show his prowess, but he is simply moving the drama along. Othello is on the verge of a far greater 'battle'.

When Laurence Olivier played Othello, he gave an interesting twist to the scene when he came onstage to curb the riot in Cyprus: he grabbed one of the rioters and throttled him. Olivier improvised to kill this rioter by breaking his neck. Great touch! But it is incongruous to me, because Othello is always very judicious. Unless we can dramatize the peaceful, married Othello in contrast to the warlike Othello, we are going to end up getting the fire going in the wrong places; and we see Othello the husband in rapture as he greets his wife when he safely reaches Cyprus. She is his 'soul's joy', his 'fair warrior', the core of his absolute content and comfort.

Later, Othello gives a stirring farewell oration to 'glorious' war:

Farewell the tranquil mind, farewell content:
Farewell the plumed troop, and the big wars,
That makes ambition virtue: O farewell,

> Farewell the neighing steed, and the shrill trump,
> The spirit-stirring drum, the ear-piercing fife,
> The royal banner, and all quality,
> Pride, pomp, and circumstance of glorious war!
> (Act III, scene iii)

For all the conviction and sincerity of his rhetoric, I do not believe for a moment that Othello loves war more than he loves Desdemona. He is simply saying farewell to all the trappings that have defined for him the experience of the warrior.

So Othello's peace, content and comfort will not last long. That is all about to change, and in that change lies the crux of the drama, and of Othello's fall and his tragedy. How to explain it? Many productions focus on jealousy. A jealous Othello, after all, fits in well with the traditions of the classical play. Yet to simply play a jealous Othello is to convey a foolish Othello. As I have said, I do not think it is jealousy that leads to Othello's ruin; I believe it is insanity born of profound confusion.

Shakespeare wrote a play about jealousy, but *Othello* isn't it. That play is *A Winter's Tale*, and it depicts pure jealousy. The only pure jealousy you will find in *Othello* permeates Iago. You find a petulant jealousy in Roderigo, but an undiluted, all-consuming jealousy in Iago. I contend that Othello never gets jealous, but is ensnared in a profound confusion that ultimately drives him quite mad.

His tragic mistake is to trust Iago more than he trusts himself. Othello is confronted with two images of his wife: the woman Iago describes and the woman he himself knows. He trusts Iago's representation of Desdemona more than he trusts his own perception of her. It is not so much that Othello fails to trust Desdemona: he does not trust himself and his faith in her; and he has no grounds to mistrust her. That's the most painful part of the whole story – mistrust Desdemona over what? When was there even time for her to be unfaithful?

Jealousy is a very tenuous theme to sustain in the play, but many productions make it the focus. The traditional emphasis on the theme of jealousy has, on occasion, kept a great actor from playing Othello. Sidney Poitier has told me that, in earlier years, when he declined to play the role, his decision was incorrectly interpreted to mean that he did not want to portray a black man as a dupe. In reality, Sidney says, he did not want to immerse himself in a role that might require him to play jealousy night after night – that jealousy is a dangerous, destructive emotion to carry around with you, onstage or in life.

Jealousy is a disease of the imagination. Harold C. Goddard writes in *The Meaning of Shakespeare* about the psychology of jealousy, and the great force of jealousy when it is aroused in a person who is *not* easily jealous. Goddard notes that it is the best qualities in Othello's nature – 'his love, his imagination, his lack of suspicion, his modesty' – that 'give Iago his chance'.[*] Goddard compares Shakespeare's depiction of Othello, the older husband of a young wife, to the true-life story of Feodor Dostoevsky and his younger wife. When Dostoevsky became jealous of his wife, he felt trapped. He could not go to his beloved and ask her if she had or had not betrayed him. That question in itself is a breach of trust, an act of betrayal. If the beloved is innocent, you can never heal the wound that question will cause. You destroy the relationship. You can't win.

That idea is supported by Dostoevsky, and by Shakespeare in *The Winter's Tale*. Leontes, the King of Sicilia, invites Polixenes, the neighbouring king, who is also his best friend,

* Goddard, 88.

to come to visit. Leontes keeps insisting that Polixenes prolong his visit, but Polixenes declines, until Leontes' wife Hermione innocently joins in her husband's invitation. Polixenes stays, and Leontes begins to say to himself, 'What have I done? I've put my wife and this gorgeous man together.' Leontes is trapped in the throes of a very modern jealousy (perhaps Oedipal?). He himself has arranged matters so that the wife he really loves and his best friend will spend time together. The minute he sees them together, however, he believes that they are bound to be lovers, and his jealousy explodes. The Freudians would say that he unconsciously set up his wife with his best friend. When he realizes it, he becomes angry at everything, including himself.

As he gives Hermione's hand to Polixenes, Leontes speaks in an aside:

> Too hot, too hot!
> To mingle friendship far is mingling bloods.
> I have tremor cordis on me; my heart dances,
> But not for joy, not joy. This entertainment
> May a free face put on; derive a liberty
> From heartiness, from bounty, fertile bosom,
> And well become the agent.

> (*The Winter's Tale*, Act I, scene ii)

Leontes has *tremor cordis* – palpitations of the heart. (Shakespeare often uses the language of medicine metaphorically, and Leontes' own physician could not have given him a more accurate diagnosis.) As Isaac Asimov observed of Leontes, 'A sickness, an abnormality, makes of the genial host, without real cause, a jealous tyrant';[*] and as Goddard says, Leontes is his own Iago.[†]

---

[*] Asimov, vol. 1, 149.

[†] Goddard, 264.

I've always thought about the significance of the cultural sentiments of *Othello* – and the issue of jealousy is, to an extent, a cultural issue. (One striking example of cultural differences occurs in the reports from early Arctic explorers that, in certain Eskimo settlements, it was a matter of courtesy and hospitality for the host to offer his wife's sexual favours to an honoured guest, and that it was considered rude and insulting for a guest to decline. When a stranger heard this invitation for the first time, what was he to do – honour his own cultural conventions and so insult his host's code of honour? Accept his host's customs at the expense of his own cultural acclimatization? How should the stranger or outsider respond when what is taboo in his culture is the practice in another?) Cultural contradictions lead to cultural vulnerability – and the stranger in a society can become, as Othello puts it, 'Perplex'd in the extreme' (Act V, scene ii). Just as Iago has infected others with the poison of racism, he tries to infect Othello with the poison of confusion, and the infection is physical (*tremor cordis*) as well as psychological. Iago says so himself:

> The Moor already changes with my poison:
> Dangerous conceits are in their natures poisons,
> Which at the first are scarce found to distaste,
> But with a little act upon the blood
> Burn like the mines of sulphur ...
> Look where he comes, not poppy, nor mandragora,
> Nor all the drowsy syrups of the world
> Shall ever medicine thee to that sweet sleep
> Which thou owedst yesterday.
>
> (Act III, scene iii)

'Tremor cordis', says Leontes; 'poison', says Iago, and Iago knows the condition intimately. He predicts that never again will Othello enjoy 'sweet sleep'. There are physical repercussions to great emotional upheaval, and before our eyes Othello falls into a trance, in the grip of an epileptic seizure. He is not the only Shakespearean character to be so afflicted: Julius Caesar also had the 'falling sickness'. Iago is present when Othello collapses, and he reveals a concrete knowledge of the symptoms and manifestations of this condition. He tells a worried Cassio that

> The lethargy must have his quiet course,
> If not, he foams at mouth, and by and by
> Breaks out to savage madness.
>
> (Act IV, scene i)

This might sound like another example of Iago's misinformation, but again, I would like to consider taking Iago at his word. There is probably a long history between the general and the ensign here. Iago has probably got him out of this predicament many times before. He is not just lying to Cassio.

Could it be that some of Othello's behaviour from this moment on can be explained as part of the disorientation following the seizure, the 'savage madness'? (Savage in this usage means 'enraged'.)* There is an interesting staging of this moment in the recent London Weekend Television (LWT) modern version of *Othello*. The director seems to imply that this has happened before to John Othello. Not only do we see the onset of the seizure; we see Othello having problems with orientation before it happens, and we see the residue of it after it happens. He never fully recovers from it.

Staging Othello's epilepsy can be tricky. Wiser people than most have said that the hero should never fall into a latitude lower than the villain, so for Othello to collapse on to the ground, lower than Iago, is inappropriate; but epileptics do

---

* Honigmann, 257, note 53.

collapse. You have to make the fall just as scary as possible, so that it is taken seriously. At that point in the play, if anything gets over into the extraordinary, it can set up a lack of credibility, even generate laughter. This scene has to be frightening.

I think it should also be one of those sensitive moments for the actor playing Iago. Often Iago is trying to get a laugh when he should treat this scene very seriously, as if already aware that he has gone too far. For Iago to indulge in malevolence at this point is probably a mistake. It is more interesting to see him deeply concerned and functioning as he probably has before, as a nurse. The actor playing Othello has to collapse. The actor playing Iago has to treat this incident delicately. He should be thinking, 'At what point is Othello going to wake up? What is he going to do then? What do I do now? It's not in the bag.'

When Othello does awaken, he challenges Iago: 'Dost thou mock me?' We have to do all we can to give this moment some size. The suspicion that haunts Othello in the throes of his confusion has got to be played for all it's worth. Othello is sensitive to something. He is picking up some signals that disturb him, but it should not be something inappropriate that Iago has demonstrated to the audience.

Apparently, at some point during Margaret Webster's landmark production of *Othello* starring Paul Robeson, Uta Hagen and Jose Ferrer, Uta said to Paul, in essence, 'You've got to be careful, especially when you do the fainting scene where you have the epileptic seizure, not to let Iago be taller than you on the stage.'

I wondered how Othello could collapse with epilepsy and still be taller than Iago; but Uta was echoing a concept of the literal as well as the symbolic supremacy of the hero in English theatre. A lot of British critics hate that moment: if there is any way for Othello to have an epileptic seizure standing up with dignity, they would prefer it. They can't deal with having the hero collapse. They say, 'This is wrong. This was not Shakespeare's intention. Give him petit mal epilepsy, not grand mal. Just say, "He nodded off a bit."'

It is after Othello's trance that Desdemona becomes his victim. He starts abusing her vocally and physically; and depending on how the epilepsy scene has been played, one may draw the conclusion that the epilepsy or the trauma going on within Othello actually triggers a derangement that we can see. This is the first sign of insanity. The fallout from that scene is that Othello abuses his wife in front of her relatives and the dignitaries. He's really gone. Desdemona is the first to recognize this profound confusion, this derangement. 'My lord is not my lord,' she tells Cassio. Something 'Hath puddled his clear spirit', she tells, Iago, 'and in such cases / Men's natures wrangle with inferior things, / Though great ones are the object' (Act III, scene iv).

Deep into the tragedy, there is Othello's last statement before he goes totally over the edge of sanity. It is when Othello makes the big mistake of asking his wife – as Dostoevsky asked his – whether she has been unfaithful.

'Heaven doth truly know it,' she answers (Act IV, scene ii). She is stunned at his reply: 'Heaven truly knows, that thou art false as hell.'

Even while Desdemona speaks out of her innocence, Othello comes to the end of hoping to have his questions answered. Curiously enough, for the first time, in his distraction and his desperation, he acknowledges a colour difference. He speaks of her as a white woman, which he has not done before. He asks, 'Was this fair paper, this most goodly book, / Made to write "whore" on?' Later, when he comes to kill her, Othello says,

> ... yet I'll not shed her blood,
> Nor scar that whiter skin of hers than snow,
> And smooth, as monumental alabaster;
> Yet she must die, else she'll betray more men.
> Put out the light, and then put out the light ...
>
> (Act V, scene ii)

The issue of honour is wrapped up in this marriage – honour and unity. Othello believes that his honour is sullied by possible infidelity on her part. A sacred unity is breached. He can't adjust to it by simply saying, 'Our marriage is over.' It has to be completely ended, but not out of vengeance. It demands full closure – not divorce, but death. It is not just a killing. He absolves the marriage by resolving the life.

Unlike Shakespeare's Othello, Cinthio's seems bent on 'getting away with it'. This is in keeping with the dastardly way Othello and Iago murder Desdemona by beating her to death. Afterwards, Desdemona's family has to track Othello down, suggesting that he was trying to get away with murder. By contrast, Shakespeare's Othello is locked in such a state of morbidity that, in a way, he is already dead. Without the light of his life, Desdemona, his life is over. So we must consider that the events between the attempted assassination of Cassio and the smothering of Desdemona are about an Othello on the path to a murder-suicide. I am not sure how culture plays into this, but from the moment Othello says, 'Farewell the tranquil mind, farewell content' (Act III, scene iii), to the end of the play, there is a ritualistic tone that did not seem to be common in Venetian culture.

'That death's unnatural, that kills for loving,' Desdemona tells Othello, but to no avail. Finally he lets go. He commits a very ritualistic murder – not driven by vengefulness as we think of it, but ritual murder. He justifies his actions in an eloquent speech, and one wonders about its cultural resonance:

> It is the cause, it is the cause, my soul,
> Let me not name it to you, you chaste stars:
> It is the cause . . .
> Yet she must die, else she'll betray more men.
> Put out the light, and then put out the light . . .
> A balmy breath, that doth almost persuade
> Justice herself to break her sword . . .
>
> (Act V, scene ii)

It is a 'heavenly' sorrow he feels after the deed is done. He expects cosmic disorder in the wake of his act, no matter how just a 'cause' he has declared it to be. 'O, insupportable! O heavy hour!' he says afterwards:

> Methinks it should be now a huge eclipse
> Of sun and moon, and that the affrighted globe
> Should yawn at alteration.

This cosmic alteration, by his own hand, is the ultimate break in unity, and the final step in Othello's disintegration. (In a Russian film production of *Othello*, as if to underline this disintegration, Othello turns completely white-haired overnight after he kills Desdemona.)

Othello's speech is never more fiery than when, in a state of poetic desperation, he recognizes his journey's end. 'O vain boast,' he says, 'Who can control his fate?' Now Desdemona and Emilia are dead, and Othello's thoughts turn to 'compt' – the Day of Judgement. After he knows Desdemona is innocent he speculates:

> ... when we shall meet at compt,
> This look of thine will hurl my soul from heaven,
> And fiends will snatch at it ...

'Blow me about in winds,' he continues, 'roast me in sulphur, / Wash me in steep-down gulfs of liquid fire!' Some people point to this as more bombast and delusion, but I think Othello is only giving voice to a more desperate farewell to Desdemona and an acknowledgement of his own crime in killing her. Again, we are talking about people who are elevated, Othello in particular, and operating on a higher plane of awareness. He is imagining the suffering that he deserves.

The aftermath of Desdemona's death is very difficult, because there is madness all around, continuing to the very end of the play – insanity; attempts to evoke vengeance. There are some great, great speeches in the final scene. Unless one is very careful, they can seem incongruous. Onstage, the simpler those moments are, the better, because once you underline what it's about – the insanity – you've got to let that carry the action. The finale of the play is overwritten as it is, and any overacting jeopardizes its credibility.

It's as if Othello has taken ritual and used it to descend into hell. After he kills Desdemona, it's as if he is using ritual to climb back until he becomes himself again. The crucial point is that Othello is struggling to redeem something of value in his life; and then there is his final, quite beautiful speech, that takes care of itself:

> Soft you, a word or two:
> I have done the state some service, and they know't;
> No more of that: I pray you in your letters,
> When you shall these unlucky deeds relate,
> Speak of them as they are; nothing extenuate,

Nor set down aught in malice; then must you speak
Of one that lov'd not wisely, but too well:
Of one not easily jealous, but being wrought,
Perplex'd in the extreme; of one whose hand,
Like the base Indian, threw a pearl away,
Richer than all his tribe; of one whose subdued eyes,
Albeit unused to the melting mood,
Drops tears as fast as the Arabian trees
Their medicinal gum; set you down this,
And say besides, that in Aleppo once,
Where a malignant and a turban'd Turk
Beat a Venetian, and traduc'd the state,
I took by the throat the circumcised dog,
And smote him thus.

    (Act V, scene ii)

Othello stabs himself, then kisses Desdemona and dies 'upon a kiss'.

Directors have to use effective stagecraft to resolve the issue of where Othello gets the weapon to kill himself. Olivier had a trick dagger affixed to his wrist, and we saw it earlier in the play; he used that dagger to lacerate his jugular. In the production of *Othello* directed by Gladys Vaughan, I had an understudy (a black actor – a silent Moor – a brother Moor?). Gladys couldn't afford to just let him sit backstage, so she brought him onstage with me as a second Moor. It worked in a very interesting way. She justified it by the reference that Iago makes to Othello's brother:

I have seen the cannon,
When it hath . . . from his very arm
Puff'd his own brother . . .

    (Act III, scene iv)

She liked the idea that Othello had a brother, and maybe more than one.

In Gladys's production, the second Moor was always onstage when Othello was there. It didn't distract in any way. It worked well to give Othello that shadow companion – a shadow of his former culture; and when, at the end of the play, it is time for Othello to kill himself, it is the brother who hands him the sword.

The Tragedy of Emilia

> Good gentlemen, let me have leave to speak,
> 'Tis proper I obey him, but not now:
> Perchance, Iago, I will ne'er go home.
>
> Emilia to Montano, Gratiano, Othello and Iago (Act V, scene ii)

Another hard matter to resolve in *Othello* is the issue of the station of women in Shakespeare's time. I think it's important for a woman to weigh in on that as director or actor; and there is more than one woman in the play. There is Emilia, Iago's wife, who is sometimes played as if she were the equivalent of Juliet's nurse; but this is not the case. Often the choice to make Emilia a dolt is to take care of what seems to be her insensitivity to crisis. But why reduce the character to accommodate what may well be a flaw in the text? (The stage directions call for Emilia to be onstage almost throughout Act III, scene iv; therefore there is no way she cannot see everything that is going on.)

Like Desdemona, Emilia is a wife with problems in her marriage. Look at the set-up: Iago at some point has become jealous of his wife – that is quite clear. But how did it happen? I get very concerned when it is allowed that Othello probably took Emilia to bed with him and Iago found out. That's too easy. I'd rather see Iago infected by the same kind of unwarranted jealousy that he's trying to implant in others.

Emilia's adultery can't be proven, but it appears that Iago is involved in an act of revenge anyway. We find nothing in the way any of the characters relate to each other or talk to each other to suggest that such an episode has actually taken place.

It is a red herring for Iago to live with. It keeps him up at night as a symptom. Somebody started this rumour, and Iago suffers for it and uses it as a stimulus for revenge. Emilia says,

> O, fie upon him! Some such squire he was,
> That turn'd your wit, the seamy side without,
> And made you to suspect me with the Moor.
> (Act IV, scene ii)

Apparently Iago has lived with this 'seamy side' for a long time.

What do the formerly Islamic Othello and the Italian Iago need to rectify this 'wrong'? The modern man would say, 'Get a divorce'; but the classic man, with his own sense of honour, would say, 'It is the cause.'

The issue of women's station is much more complex in the play. Rumours about the exploits of Venetian courtesans had drifted to Shakespeare's England, and Iago alludes to those contemporary images when he tells Othello that even Venetian ladies who are married have certain propensities: 'In Venice they do let God see the pranks / They dare not show their husbands . . .' (Act III, scene iii).

Iago might even suggest that all women are that way. He challenges all positive concepts of what women stand for. He refers to the 'super-subtle' Venetian women who like variety and change (Act I, scene iii). Othello is not a Venetian; he has not been raised in that society. What's he to know? Is it true? And by Act IV Othello himself is calling his wife 'that cunning whore of Venice' (Act IV, scene ii).

Emilia harbours a crucial piece of information about the 'evidence' – the handkerchief. This token is a source of endless confusion, with terrible consequences. It has been a gift to Desdemona from Othello. When he suffers a headache, in Act III, scene iii, she attempts to soothe him by binding his head with the handkerchief. (The 'pain upon my forehead' is often taken to mean: 'I feel cuckold's horns growing on my forehead.' I think it is obtuse to suggest that Othello means this.) 'Your napkin is too little,' Othello tells her, and she drops it to the floor. They are both distracted, and they exit together, leaving behind the handkerchief. Emilia retrieves the handkerchief. She tell us that this was Desdemona's 'first remembrance from the Moor', that Desdemona loves it, that Othello 'conjured' her to keep it always, and that she keeps it with her all the time 'To kiss, and talk to'. Furthermore, according to Emilia, Iago has a 'hundred times wooed' her to steal it.

Devoted as she appears to be to Desdemona, and aware as she is of the significance of this token, Emilia decides to give it to Iago anyway. She says to herself, '. . . what he'll do with it / Heaven knows, not I'; but she keeps silent about what she has done, and she lies when Desdemona asks her where she might have lost her handkerchief. Disconcerted, Emilia responds, 'I know not, madam' (Act III, scene iv). Emilia is in such a fix that most likely, when she is asked a question, she has to think it through before she can answer; she has to edit herself so that the wrong thing doesn't come out. She is highly sensitized to the point of panic, or else she is a dolt.

The handkerchief continues to generate confusion, if not deceit. Emilia keeps mum about its whereabouts. Desdemona does not confess to Othello that it is missing, and both of them seem to have forgotten the moment when Othello refused it because it was too small. Othello tells Desdemona a story about the handkerchief that she has not heard before, and I certainly want to take Othello's word for it: an Egyptian gave it to his mother, he says; there was 'magic in the web of it'; it was dangerous to lose it.

'I'faith, is't true?' Desdemona asks. Othello wants to know where the handkerchief is, and demands to see it. Desdemona says she will fetch it, but not now. She continues to press her case for Cassio's reinstatement. Othello keeps asking for the handkerchief. Emilia is present for the whole conversation, and she doesn't say a word! Only when it is too late, after Desdemona's death, does Emilia comprehend the whole truth.

There is a telling moment between Emilia and Iago that demonstrates how desperate and rattled Iago is. It comes in Act V, scene ii when he pulls his knife on Emilia to make her keep silent. This must have been his habitual tactic with her. He has always made her shut up somehow, whether through male power or spousal abuse, I don't know; but he has silenced her in profoundly frightening ways, almost to the point where she is spiritually and emotionally lobotomized. There is something highly tense about Emilia. Whereas Iago is rattled and is improvising out of his desperation, Emilia is constantly traumatized. I conjecture that she has been abused in some way. Iago might not ever have struck her physically, but something has happened. Something has snapped in him. She is aware of it; she doesn't know what to do with it, and it terrifies her. She sees the devil cut loose. Emilia can't call her husband a devil, but she sees it happen.

As Desdemona watches Othello sink deeper into his confusion, his despair and his insanity, Emilia still seems unaware until the bitter end of Iago's role in Othello and Desdemona's misery. One of the most sensitive scenes between Emilia and Desdemona has to be the one in Act IV, scene iii when Emilia is preparing Desdemona's bed. (With foreknowledge of the play, we understand what they don't: that it is her death bed.) Desdemona never shrinks from what she's got herself into; though she does appeal to Iago to go to Othello and find out what is wrong, Desdemona never turns the responsibility for her fate over to anyone else. When Othello instructs her to go to bed and dismiss her servant, Emilia expresses some alarm, but Desdemona is willing to take it on. 'I would you had never seen him!' Emilia says. 'So would not I,' Desdemona replies; 'my love doth so approve him / That even his stubbornness, his checks and frowns . . . have grace and favour in them.'

Then Emilia and Desdemona share a moment when Desdemona recalls a song from her childhood, and they start talking about how complex men are. It's a wonderful scene, and if the casting is right, we have in Emilia a character who is probably as close to the truth as anybody gets; but she did pick up the handkerchief, she did turn it over to Iago, and all she's done is sworn herself to silence and to secrecy. She knows, but she doesn't tell. It's very curious that she keeps that secret even though she loves Desdemona and knows what some men can be like.

You have in Emilia the totally obedient wife. It is a matter of rank, of order. She and Iago are of lower station, and Emilia doesn't have the sophistication to challenge a man as Desdemona does. Yet she has her own practical knowledge and wisdom, and her very strong opinions about men, including the issue of their fidelity, or lack of it. Desdemona, more sheltered, asks Emilia if it is true that there are women who are unfaithful to their husbands. 'Wouldst thou do such a deed for all the world?' Desdemona asks. 'The world is a huge thing, it is a great price / For a small vice,' Emilia replies. She speaks lightly, as if trying to cheer Desdemona:

> . . . marry, I would not do such a thing for a joint-ring; or for measures of lawn, nor for gowns, or petticoats, nor caps, nor any such exhibition; but for the whole world? ud's pity, who would not make her husband a cuckold to make him a monarch? I should venture purgatory for it.

Yet Desdemona insists that she would not do her husband wrong 'For the whole world'.

Then Emilia gives a remarkably outspoken speech about marriage, and one that would have been unorthodox, if not shocking, in its time. She tells Desdemona that if 'wives do fall', the blame goes to their husbands. Wives 'have their palates both for sweet, and sour, / As husbands have,' Emilia says, and she continues:

And have not we affections?
Desires for sport? and frailty, as men have?
Then let them use us well: else let them know,
The ills we do, their ills instruct us so.

This is a woman who could have rationalized letting Othello into her bed but for her fear of Iago.

However, Desdemona never wavers in her loyalty to Othello, or in her defence of him, in contrast to Emilia, who wavers but does not expose Iago. She can't let go of her sense of obedience. She can't cross him, until it is too late. This can be perceived as a weakness on Emilia's part. What Desdemona is going through cannot be perceived as a weakness. She will not do anything but give Othello the benefit of the doubt. She will not hold him to blame, even when she is dying. When they ask, 'Who did this to you?' she says, 'Nobody, I myself' (Act V, scene ii).

Yet Emilia is not simply a counterpoint to the lyricism and grace of Desdemona. She is not just a boorish, diminished, dismissible minor character; she is more than that. She eventually becomes the heroine of the play. She avenges Desdemona, at the price of her own life. It is too late, but she does ultimately come through with the truth. She exposes Othello and Iago. Once again, Iago tries to silence her, but she refuses to be silenced, begging liberty to break the usual order of the wife's subservience to her husband. 'Good gentlemen,' she pleads, 'let me have leave to speak, / 'Tis proper

I obey him, but not now' (Act V, scene ii). As Iago threatens her, she protests:

I'll be in speaking, liberal as the air,
Let heaven, and men, and devils, let 'em all,
All, all cry shame against me, yet I'll speak.

She reveals everything. That side of Emilia should not come as a surprise. That potential should be there in the way Emilia is cast and in the way she plays the part. And for the tragedy of Emilia, there is redemption in her final words:

Moor, she was chaste, she lov'd thee, cruel Moor,
So come my soul to bliss as I speak true;
So speaking as I think, I die, I die.

The Survival of Cassio

> And what was he?
> Forsooth, a great arithmetician,
> One Michael Cassio, a Florentine . . .
>
> Iago to Roderigo (Act I, scene i)

Michael Cassio is really my favourite kind of human being in the whole play, more so than Othello. He is not unlike Horatio in *Hamlet*: a quiet, supportive friend. He is a handsome Florentine, a gentleman of quality and a dutiful, obedient lieutenant who has no agenda of his own but to sustain his honour. Cassio and Othello have apparently known each other for a long time, and they are devoted friends. Cassio is also devoted to Desdemona, whom he respects and reveres. Cassio keeps company with Othello and Desdemona and is, like each of them, an evolved human being. You can hear it in the poetry of his speech.

There is some mystery about Cassio's personal life, perhaps because, as some suggest, Shakespeare left it a loose end in the tapestry of the play. As Iago tells it, Cassio is 'A fellow almost damn'd in a fair wife' (Act I, scene i). People have puzzled across the centuries about this single reference to Cassio's wife in the play, especially in the face of the very real presence of Cassio's mistress, the courtesan Bianca.

Cassio possesses a flaw that leaves him vulnerable to being manipulated. I think it's more complex than his weakness for wine. He knows, as Iago does, that he has 'very poor and unhappy brains for drinking', and Cassio wishes that 'courtesy would invent some other custom of entertainment'.

He says to Iago, 'I am unfortunate in the infirmity, and dare not task my weakness with any more' (Act II, scene iii).

Cassio is a man with a conscience, and he suffers when he is stripped of his office after the debacle in the streets of Cyprus. He understands that Othello loves him, but that he has to make an example of him. Cassio mourns the loss of his reputation: 'I ha' lost my reputation! I ha lost the immortal part, sir, of myself, and what remains is bestial' (Act II, scene iii).

This is another fall from grace; but, he says, he would rather be despised 'than to deceive so good a commander, with so light, so drunken, and indiscreet an officer' as himself. He speaks eloquently of the 'devil' wine, and the 'devil drunkenness' that gives rise to 'the devil wrath'. 'O God,' he says, 'that men should put an enemy in their mouths, to steal away their brains; that we should with joy, revel, pleasure, and applause, transform ourselves into beasts!'

He is a man who takes responsibility for his actions, and whose friendship and loyalty do not waver. 'Bounteous madame,' he says to Desdemona as he asks her to intercede for him with Othello, 'Whatever shall become of Michael Cassio, / He's never anything but your true servant' (Act III, scene iii). As Harold C. Goddard has written of him, Cassio is 'the profligate with a pure heart, the drunkard who comes through true as steel'.* By the end of the drama, in the wake of Othello's tragedy, he has been elevated to the governorship of Cyprus.

Unlike the stories of Othello, Desdemona, Iago and Emilia, Cassio's personal story does not end in tragedy. He has time to account for himself. Cassio survives.

* Goddard, 75.

Productions of Othello

I will a round unvarnish'd tale deliver . . .

Othello to the Duke and the Senate (Act I, scene iii)

Somebody has said, 'You can't play King Lear until you're sixty.' Well, I believe you should start playing Lear or Hamlet or Othello when you are sixteen. You start early to look at the wonder and mystery of the Shakespearean play, as if it were a mountain – or a great block of marble. As Michelangelo said when he began a new sculpture, the figure is in the stone. The Lear or Othello or Hamlet you hope to evoke lurks in the play, like a figure in the stone. You ask yourself, 'Where do I carve and sculpt?' You hope to cut into the very core of the rock, to lure the figure out of the stone.

I think that each new generation has to have a crack at all the great plays. The mission of the actor in each generation is to keep exploring a great mountain of a play such as *Othello* until he finds its heart. Hopefully, we will learn something valuable to pass on to future generations; but we have to keep chipping away at the stone, creatively and honestly, with good faith.

That's the job of the actor, and that's what Campbell Scott did with his recent motion picture production of *Hamlet*. It is not a matter of competition. It is not a matter of trying to stage *Hamlet* better than his father, George C. Scott, has done. It's not about whether you can do a better *Othello* than your predecessors, or whether Liev Schreiber can do a funnier Iago than Christopher Plummer. It's about chipping and sculpting away with honesty and integrity, to see if you can discover the play again; or, perhaps, discover it for the first time ever.

In the fall of 1955, as a student in the American Theater Wing in New York, I was assigned to work on Hotspur's speech in *King Henry IV, Part One*. I was staying at my father's apartment then, and he is an actor, too. When he saw me working on Hotspur, he decided to introduce me to Othello, a role he has performed twice in workshop productions. 'If you are going to play Othello,' my father said, 'you have to really clean up your act, even spiritually. You have to come to him strong and clean.' He emphasized Othello's nobility of presence and soul. He was saying, 'You can best portray a quality by possessing the quality, at least for the duration of that role. If the character has one nature, you can't indulge in the opposing nature.'

I first played Othello at the Manistee Summer Theater in Michigan in 1956, when I was twenty-five. In that production I got to wear the suede boots worn by William Marshall when he played Othello in 1953.[*] When I examine the productions I've been involved with, I see that in this first one I did not yet understand the magnitude of Shakespeare's concept of love. That summer in Michigan I fell in love with the actress who played Desdemona. What I learned from that experience is that loving the actress does not help the play, and it did not help me achieve the role of Othello. If anything, this offstage relationship gets in the way. You become self-conscious, and a key to this play is that Shakespeare, as I've said, is dealing in genuine love – not just romantic or sexual or Freudian love, but passionate love, sacred love.

From that first production I also learned that Othello has a great many lines – more dialogue than I had ever recited on stage in my life up to that moment, and Bill Marshall's boots

---

[*] William Marshall later played in *Catch My Soul*, a rock musical version of *Othello*, also starring Julienne Marie and Jerry Lewis. This was made into a film with Richie Havens as Othello, Lance LeGault as Iago and Season Hubley as Desdemona.

didn't help. Then I learned I was 'lucky', because Iago had even more lines than Othello.

It is totally ridiculous to do Shakespeare in summer stock when you only have a week to rehearse. You hope that by opening night you know your lines, and that's about as far as you can get – but it is a beginning. I've always marvelled at the actors of other cultures, especially of Britain: how Peter O'Toole had a chance to play Shylock when he was twenty-five years old; how Christopher Plummer was doing King John in Canada when he was twenty-five. The great virtue of having the Shakespearean legacy in your culture is that young actors get a chance to act in the plays earlier and more frequently.

I worked on Othello with Tad Danielewski in his workshop in New York, and learned from him two important concepts: first, the actor's prime task is to assess the character's intention. Second, to do that, the actor must deal with the evidence the playwright gives him; we must carefully probe the text of the play – in other words, ask: What is Othello up to? And what evidence does Shakespeare give us in the text?

Tad explained that to build Othello you first have to unbuild him, according to the clues in the language of the play. He told me that, while Othello was a great general, that was not what he had set out to do with his life. His purpose was not to be a great warrior, according to Tad. Instead, Othello desired peace and love – respite from chaos. He desired progeny. Tad believed that this idea is supported by the text, and often totally ignored, because people have other agendas. 'The fountain, from the which my current runs, / Or else dries up . . .' (Act IV, scene ii) – that is one reason Othello marries Desdemona. He seems to say that with this woman he will create a new generation. It is part of his life's mission.*

* Jones and Niven, 147–8.

I began to understand that when Othello arrives in Venice, he sees what he has missed since he left his family's palace as a child. He wants the peace of a civilized life, not the chaos of war. Desdemona and her love give him this peace. To lose Desdemona is to fall again into chaos. To lose her is to lose himself.

Beginning in the summer of 1960, I was fortunate to work in Joe Papp's New York Shakespeare Festival. I played small roles in several productions, and was cast as Oberon in *A Midsummer Night's Dream*, the Prince of Morocco in *The Merchant of Venice*, Caliban in *The Tempest*, and Macduff in the Scottish play. Thanks to this experience, I was growing more at home in Shakespeare's language as well as within his characters.

In the summer of 1963 I got my second chance to play Othello, this time in another summer stock production, at the Corning Summer Theater in Corning, New York, with Dorothy Chernuck directing. Two interesting things happened: first, the actor playing Iago had other roles to learn that summer as the major actor in the company, the leading man. He and the director said, 'Let's record Iago's soliloquies, so that when other characters are onstage he will talk directly to them, and when he is by himself the audience will hear his soundtrack.'

Some people think Iago is talking to the audience, but I don't think it's that simple. He is ruminating, very much as Hamlet does. (In fact, I believe there is a very strong kinship between Hamlet and Iago.) The recording was an interesting experiment, but it didn't work because Shakespeare didn't write the soliloquy for the electronic age. He wrote it for the actor to speak the words out loud, or 'aside', in person.

The director attempted a second innovation: because we had a small budget, we decided to do the play in modern dress, as if we were all modern 'mercenary' soldiers; we were dressed like Green Berets. There are references in the play such as

'Keep up your bright swords', but we were outfitted with guns as well as swords. When you've got a .45 strapped to your waist and you carry a sword and you are supposed to kill somebody, what's the point of drawing your sword? Modern dress can present serious problems in a production of Shakespeare's plays if you are using Shakespeare's text. In Richard Burton's *Hamlet*, Gertrude was resplendent in a modern mink coat, and certainly fur was in the royal wardrobe of the time, but with this style of coat, she just looked as if she was cold all the time. If you step out of time with costumes, you have to be sure to give the audience every stitch and inch of cultural context to help them understand the time of the play. Otherwise you risk depriving them of the atmosphere that helps explain so much of why people behave as they do in the play. The Corning production of *Othello* confronted the audience with the Iago sound track and the modern wardrobe and the total inability to evoke another culture or cultures.

Later in 1963 I made my first trip to Venice, involved in an entirely different project; but suddenly Othello caught up with me. One day, my gondolier pointed towards a building in the bend of a canal. 'This is the castle of Otello,' he said. I was sceptical; I thought, 'This guy surely knows how to get a tip from a black tourist!' But he was emphatic. 'Otello was a character in an Italian novella. The novelist patterned Otello after a Moorish general who used to live here. Otello – Little Otto.'

My time in Venice brought me intuitively closer to Othello; and that Christmas of 1963 brought me terrific news: Joe Papp wanted to cast me as Othello in the New York Shakespeare Festival production in the summer of 1964. It was directed by Gladys Vaughan. Mitchell Ryan was a wonderful Iago. He and I were similar in temperament and 'type'. We even had the same zodiac sign. The only difference was that he was

Caucasian and I was African. The characters were like brothers and that worked surprisingly well. It created an instant bond between the two men. Iago and Othello are often cast as a bulldog and a bear; Iago is a wiry little guy bringing down the giant bear. The play works best when both Othello and Iago are strong men, both totally heterosexual and totally credible as soldiers. In this production, you saw two men capable of being soldiers who loved each other like brothers.

I think Gladys did let Mitchell explore a little bit of Freudian nonsense. When he kills Roderigo, he kisses him at the same time. That gesture veers toward something Freudian or emotional or romantic, but Gladys was curious about what's really going on with Iago. At the same time, she made sure that the role of Desdemona was realized in a way that is not easy, because it is underwritten. All the female characters in Shakespeare were underwritten because they were played by boys with more limited stage experience and certainly no experience at being women. In a way, Shakespeare had to write the women in shorthand.

The actress playing Desdemona is almost always best served by a woman director. The whole play is. The average American male director, and probably British male directors as well, have certain problems: they can't really get over the idea that if your wife is unfaithful, you should dump her. 'Get a divorce,' they seem to say automatically. 'What's the big problem?'

Or, if they are looking at *Measure for Measure*, they tend to say, 'So the Deputy Duke wants you to sleep with him just to save your brother's life. What's the big problem? It's your brother's life you're talking about.' They can't acknowledge that the girl – the sister in that case – intends to marry Jesus. She is a novice nun. The average American male would say, 'What's the problem?' That is underneath the male thinking, especially in a time of cynicism.

In Margaret Webster's landmark production of *Othello* starring Paul Robeson, Uta Hagen and Jose Ferrer, there was the ironic benefit that World War II was going on. There was admiration for and reliance on generals, and more understanding of what generals did, just as there is now in the present crisis begun by September 11. The contemporary idea of Robeson's general walking onstage garnering immediate respect was helpful to the production; but to perform *Othello*, as we did, during the Vietnam era was much harder.

Furthermore, we were performing in a volatile political time, with widespread racial tension and 'black rage'. Joe Papp suggested that Othello should be tough and militant in order to be an exciting dramatic hero. Gladys, on the contrary, insisted on a portrayal of Othello the noble, graceful hero – a sun god, a superior, benevolent being. She encouraged me to think of Desdemona as the 'dis-demon', the anti-demon, and of Iago as Lucifer, the beautiful fallen angel.* Like Tad Danielewski, she emphasized that we had to examine the text of the play and base our interpretations on the evidence in the text. She taught us that each character leans on the other characters. In *Othello*, the drama is supported by three pillars – Othello, Iago and Desdemona. Each pillar must carry great weight, or the drama begins to collapse.

Most of all, my experience with Gladys taught me the difference a good director can make in a production. Only a good director can lead actors – and the audience – through the intense and painful journey of dramatic tragedy to a safe landing on the other side. As I have observed before, Shakespeare's plays are infused with archaic laws and values, and women directors seem better equipped to get at those universal, timeless themes.

* Jones and Niven, 159.

The Shakespeare in the Park production had the advantage of being played outside. In the spacious outdoors, it gained size and magnitude. After its scheduled run in the summer of 1964, the production opened in the Martinique Theater in New York on 12 October 1964 and ran for 224 performances. The small theatre was not a disadvantage, compared to the outdoor staging: it gave us a pressure-cooker effect. It was very, very strong because the audience was totally involved in the play.

By that time I was quite aware of my attraction to Desdemona – Julienne Marie. I did not marry my Desdemona, however, until after she had left the production and was on her way to do the rock version of *Othello* in Los Angeles.

My next excursion into *Othello* came in 1968 when I was asked to play the role in a student production at the Goodman Theater in Chicago. Len Cariou would play Iago. Here, also, Iago was played by a man who had a similar temperament to mine.

I remember that, in one rehearsal, the director could not get the young student actress playing Desdemona to cry. That should not be a director's task anyway; he defines the character for you and suggests how best to get at it. Having Desdemona weep was probably irrelevant, but when the director couldn't get her to cry, he slapped her. That is an example of when a cast and a director are out of sync. I felt that Len and I were in sync, but we were older and somewhat more experienced than the rest of the cast – and that much more professional, frankly. There were actors in that production who went on to great things, including George Dzundza of *Law and Order* fame, and Carrie Snodgress, who did *Diary of a Mad Housewife*.

Aside from Gladys Vaughan's, the production that I think was the most telling was the 1971 *Othello* at the Mark Taper Forum in Los Angeles, with John Berry directing. By then, John and I had worked well together in the movie *Claudine*, and in the theatre productions of *Les Blancs* and Athol Fugard's *The Blood Knot* and *Boesman and Lena*.

As the director, John's first consideration was: 'How should we cast the play?' Jill Clayburgh, who was very much in demand at the time, was cast as Desdemona. John was torn between asking Stacy Keach or Tony Zerba to play Iago. Stacy's star was on the rise, but John was worried that he might not be able to resist all the 'star turn' potential with Iago. John went with Tony; but the problem with Tony and me was that we had recently done the play elsewhere.

John was then married to the young woman who had been the stage manager for Gladys Vaughan's production. It's my hunch that she told John to watch out in case I played Othello as Gladys had directed me, and that she warned him that Tony was still too close to the production he had recently performed in San Diego. I felt that John's wife began to affect our production by making him insecure about his directions. He worried that he had two actors who were sabotaging him by sticking to their old interpretations of the play.

For whatever reason, something was clearly not working between Iago and me. At one point I remember lying on a bench in frustration, and I said only to myself, 'I've got to stand up and say, "Let's stop this. Let's do *King Lear* instead of *Othello*."' It would not have been too late to make the change, but I didn't have the time to think it through, or the courage to suggest it, so I continued with *Othello*.

When the play opened, it got mixed reviews, but Jill Clayburgh's Desdemona was not well received by the critics. Offstage, it was common knowledge in Hollywood that Jill and Al Pacino had just broken up. She was not looking for a replacement love, but she was understandably fragile. She needed to be taken care of, and in our play no one was taking care of anybody. Without a woman director, that can happen. When the critics came down on Jill, it was devastating.

Ironically, though, a throng of young students in Los Angeles came to see the play just because it was Shakespeare, and it became a sell-out. Soon the critics came back and said, 'Oh, they're selling out. They must have improved the production.' Now they rewrote reviews, saying that we had improved mightily. The critics tried to figure out why the production could be successful when they had panned it. We owed our surprising success to the curiosity of the young people of Los Angeles. They simply wanted to see some Shakespeare.

Tony Zerba is a great poetic actor. He and Roscoe Lee Brown have toured a programme of poetry that was just astonishing. So students were given a feast when they came to see this American actor doing Shakespeare. I was undergoing primal therapy at the time, so I was caught between great depression and despair. John Berry and I were old friends from off-Broadway days. John and I had everything but trust going between us; we loved each other. If he had played Iago, I think he and I might have achieved something of what Tony and I missed. It was not that Tony was on the wrong track with his portrayal of Iago. It was that Tony and I were not sharing the same track – not like Mitchell Ryan and I or Len Cariou and I shared the same track.

The main problem for John was that it was his return to Hollywood. He had been blacklisted during the McCarthy period and he wanted to return in triumph. Well, the critics took care of that, and in a way we all took care of that by not getting the play on track.

I recall the day when John wanted to evoke some passion from the actor playing Brabantio. He was a star on some sitcom, I think, one of those mature, grey-haired gentlemen.

John wanted him to convey the outrage that Shakespeare wrote for Desdemona's father, but the actor, with too many years of television, didn't know where to go for that passion.

I remember John saying, 'We've got to do something with that text,' and the actor said, 'No, that's it. That's what you get.' The actor was saying to the director, 'That's all you get because that's what you do in television, you know. I've got my lines – what more do you expect?' John eventually replaced that actor, but too late. He found an actor who had a political history similar to his – that kind of deep political passion. It was better, but it didn't help that much.

John and I never took a stab at one unusual concept, because it would have meant disrupting the rehearsal process and the production. John thought Othello was a cynic, just as Iago is a cynic. John had worked in North Africa as a film director, and he expressed his opinion that you encounter some scary cynicism in many Islamic people. He interpreted it as a macho thing with Arab men. He suggested that we had to explore that cynicism in Othello. At what point does Othello become more cynical than Iago?

The idea that Othello is a cynic is intriguing, but it would take a vanity production to make this perspective work. By vanity I mean that a cynical Othello is now going to go for more laughs than Iago gets in some productions. Vanity productions can, of course, be fun and expedient, and can exploit the particular strengths of the cast. I am not condemning them, but they do not necessarily allow you to get the best production of the play. You can offer an unusual interpretation, for example by playing Iago as a woman, or as a black man, or by having one actor play both Othello and Iago.

I am sure that the 'edge' that Joe Papp wanted with the black militant interpretation and John Berry's concept of cynicism were valuable, and to some degree would enrich the character; but I have to observe that if slavery didn't throw Othello off his nature, how could anger or disenchantment do it?

When I saw Errol John do his production of *Othello* in London, it was as if he was looking behind his back the whole time. He gave us an Othello who was aware that Iago was trying to manipulate his mind. Errol was racially defensive in real life, and brought racial defensiveness onstage. Othello cannot be defensive. To reiterate: Othello is a prince. He has not experienced the second-class-citizen syndrome. What does he know about personal or institutional racism?

This brings me to the production that became the 'bloody farce' – the production that was directed by Peter Coe. It began in Stratford, Connecticut, in 1981, and then moved to the Winter Garden Theater in February of 1982. I played Othello and Christopher Plummer played Iago, in an interpretation of the play that seemed to have been borrowed from Thomas Rymer, the seventeenth-century critic who called the play a 'bloody farce' and pronounced Othello a 'booby'.

If the play turns towards farce, Othello can be reduced to foolishness. I am convinced that Othello can at no time be aware of Iago's duplicity. Roderigo can possibly be aware, and Cassio can eventually be aware, but never Othello. Therefore the director and the actor playing Iago bear a certain responsibility for making sure that Othello is never aware of the deception. The audience is aware only because Iago lets them in on the secret; but it flat out doesn't work to do that in Othello's presence, or in the presence of any character whom Iago is out to deceive. If Iago is a farcical villain, then Othello becomes a farcical hero, and this great tragic drama is perverted into a farce. I cannot accept this as Shakespeare's intention.

The character of Othello does not deserve laughter in the midst of his deepest trauma. Laughter from the audience does not come out of nowhere. The audience's perception that the play is a farce comes only after a certain perception that something is not credible. If an actor isn't up to a role, it can become a parody. The audience will scoff at what is being portrayed, and they will go into laughter. Then you might as well give the audience their money back and go home, or possibly just unzip your fly, drop your hose and join in the fun.

In this 1981–2 production, unfortunately, at every stop, beginning in Stratford, where we originated, continuing in most of the towns where we played, and then finally on Broadway, Chris as Iago generated laughter at certain points in the drama. He was probably as frustrated and surprised by that laughter as anyone was, but he seemed to exploit it. As I recall, Chris said to me in Minneapolis, 'Jimmy, this play is a bloody farce after all,' as if to say, 'I'm sorry, I just can't take it seriously.' He probably wasn't looking for a farce, but he found one.

At the time, Chris was starring in *Henry V*, and working doubly hard. He has been an accomplished Shakespearean actor since he was in his twenties. The earlier Chris Plummer could walk onstage so deeply involved in his character that the audience would forget to give him the obligatory entrance applause. This was the case with *Royal Hunt of the Sun* (1965–6) in which Chris starred as Pizarro. The later Chris Plummer appeared to enjoy the star turn, when he could walk onstage to immediate applause of recognition and appreciation, as in his wonderful performance as John Barrymore (1997).

Some actors approach the play as farce, and I felt that this was what Chris did under Peter Coe's direction. A good director will guide the actor into the tragedy. Iago's cynicism should not infect the audience simply as amusement. There were other moments that evoked laughter in this production because of Peter's staging: the audience laughed at Roderigo's death, and they laughed during one of the confrontation scenes between Othello and Desdemona in which Peter wanted me to knock Desdemona to the floor. When Desdemona fell, the full, heavy skirts of her gown billowed out and she seemed to sink down into the floor. The audience laughed every time at a moment when they should have been absorbing her pain. We eliminated that particular action by Othello before we went to Broadway, but the audience still laughed at Iago.

When my wife Cecilia Hart joined the cast as the fourth Desdemona, she was determined that, because the laughs during the play were inappropriate, she was going to step on them; and she did. The other actresses playing Desdemona seemed unaware of how serious and distracting the laughter was, nor did they have the courage to intervene. I tried to squelch a few of the laughs myself. For example, in Act III, scene iii Iago provokes Othello to a crescendo of doubt, only to caution him,

O, beware jealousy;
It is the green-ey'd monster, which doth mock
That meat it feeds on.

Othello responds, 'Oh, misery,' as Iago leads him on toward chaos. At the end of this crucial scene, Chris would exit, but not by the simplest route. Instead, he would exit behind me and he would get a laugh at a moment when the play does not need a laugh. I would keep my eyes on him. In an effort to counteract this exit, I began to track Iago. I would follow him and it worked for a few performances. So then the audience was aware that I was aware of Chris's antics, and they started laughing at that moment.

Chris, though, was playing it as farce even to the end of the play. The lighting designer had thrown a spotlight on the bed in the final scene, when all the other major characters are dead. The only major character alive is Iago, and he found the spot and would revel in it: it would leave the audience laughing all the way out of the theatre; but this strategy also lays waste a whole play about human beings. When the stage is littered with bodies, what's so funny?

Young people will laugh when Romeo kisses Juliet because it embarrasses them, and they'll make kissing noises if you let them. The director has to be very careful that sudden acts of violence can jar an audience into laughter. The American habit of laughing under stress is worth a psychological study.

The only place where 'inappropriate laughter' didn't happen in our production of *Othello* was in Fort Lauderdale and most of our other stops in Florida. I finally figured that it had to do with the fact that so many New Yorkers, Canadians and British retire in Florida – Fort Lauderdale, Orlando, Palm Beach and Miami. They were knowledgeable about Shakespeare; they were good listeners. The Florida audience knew what this kind of classical play was about. They knew the culture of classical theatre. They just wouldn't laugh. It was a great pleasure playing there.

What New York expected was for Chris and me – these two so-called 'best actors in American theatre' – to 'duke it out'. Othello and Iago can't duke it out – not directly, overtly – without Othello becoming defensive, as Errol John was in his British production.

The great thing about the production we did for Gladys Vaughan in 1964 was that it was everybody's play. It wasn't Othello's play, and it wasn't Iago's play; it was everybody's play – so much so that Julienne as Desdemona probably received the best reviews. We all had great reviews, but hers were the best because the female critics got it right away. Critic Judith Crist, for example, praised Julienne's performance and observed that, for the first time, Desdemona occupied her rightful place in Shakespeare's tragedy. Desdemona is one character who is usually sloughed off in a production of *Othello*, just as Ophelia is sloughed off in *Hamlet*. Desdemona, Ophelia – all the major ingénues – often get short shrift because they are working with a male director, and he does not get it.

For the play to work to its fullest, the roles of Othello, Iago and Desdemona must be carefully balanced – three carefully calibrated 'pillars'. Each actor has a responsibility to the whole production. In 1972 the critic Jerry Tallmer reviewed the Shakespeare in the Park production of *Hamlet*, in which Stacy Keach played Hamlet, Colleen Dewhurst played Gertrude, and I played Claudius. Tallmer called his review 'I, Claudius' as a way of saying that I dominated the production. He was paying a compliment, I think, but I have wondered since if I distorted the production. There was definitely a palpable chemistry between Colleen and me as Gertrude and Claudius. I believe Stacy was fascinated by it, but he got distracted by it, I think, because he was thinking about how he could accommodate it. There is always a danger, whether you are doing good work or misguided work, of unbalancing a production.

Without a strong director who can help him, it is painful for an actor to go through tragedy. It's very painful for Iago to move through the path of his tragedy, for a more modern tragedy confronts Iago than Othello. Othello's is more classic – a grander, epic tragedy. Iago's is an everyday tragedy: somebody gets screwed over by people who hold power over him. That is a very painful and common tragedy.

We often look to the Machiavellian mould for the 'evildoers' of Shakespeare's time. There are appropriate models of 'evil-doers' from Shakespeare's era, of course, but there are more appropriate moulds in our own time, as I have suggested: from the totalitarian regimes – from Hitler's time with Goebbels as his henchman, or Stalin's time with Beria. Then there are the undercover double agents – the guys who have lived two lives. You can use the Machiavellian mould, that Iago is intentionally up to no good; but the man who is split is the victim of his own evil-doing.

In Act I, scene ii Iago swears by Janus, the Roman god of the portal, whose two faces guarded the gates to heaven, and the gates of temples in times of peace and war. Janus's face of evil doesn't just look like evil; it is evil. Somehow each of Iago's 'faces' is genuine. When he turns his loving face to you, he *is* a loving person. When the other face is there, he *is* quite different. Were Iago to deal with the unconscious Othello quite lovingly, the audience would understand the complexity of this character. They think he hates Othello, and they are quite surprised to see Iago showing love to the object of his hatred. For the actor playing Iago to take the 'split' far beyond schizophrenia is to achieve a deeper context for the play. We know that Iago is split, but to move that split from the psychological to the mythological is much richer.

There is a recent book about the double agent Robert Hanssen, *The Bureau and the Mole*. What worked for Hanssen was that he lived a secret, split life until his split worlds veered dangerously close together. He was a family man, but he never let the wild man break through; he kept that under control. He had relationships with other women, but they weren't sexual. The women were very confused by it. It was as if the animal in him knew better – knew that, once you crossed that line, it all unravels.

I want to suggest that there are other models for Iago and his calumny than Machiavelli. Shakespeare was dealing with a concept more universal than schizophrenia, which had not been scientifically articulated in his time. The idea of the double agent comes closer to it than anything. There is deep pathology in this kind of behaviour, of course, but there is still a choice. Iago, like Hanssen, the modern double agent, is responsible in both modes. Hanssen said at his sentencing to life in prison, 'I have torn the trust of so many.' Iago tears the trust of everyone he touches. He goes after his own ends heedless of the lives he destroys. Like Hanssen, he could be called 'the cruelest kind of thief', because he steals from the faith and the lives of others, all the while pretending to be trustworthy. Iago could say, as the scorpion said to the frog after he attacked him, not, 'It's my nature,' but, 'It's my job.'

However, Othello is not a bloody farce; it is a tragedy.

Peter Coe was actually quite a fan of Chris's Iago – much more than he was a fan of my Othello. As I remember it, when I told Peter that I couldn't work with him as director any more, he said, 'You're just jealous because Chris gets more laughs than you do.' Peter and I never resolved our artistic differences over *Othello*. When the play moved to Washington before going on to Broadway, Zoe Caldwell came in to direct the production, and she reshaped the whole thing. She put a stop to that moment in the last scene of the play when the final spotlight illuminated Iago reaching up into the light, revelling in his triumphs.

She almost salvaged the production with Scotch tape and Band-Aids. Early on, she recast Desdemona, bringing Dianne Wiest in to play the part. Not only is Dianne a friend, she is an actress whose talent I admire. Dianne was an ideal Desdemona. She has all the talent that this character requires. Some odd wardrobing was created, however, trying to capture the Venetian style, and this approach didn't serve her or the play. She was given big red hair and big billowy costumes, and you got no sense of the person concealed in those costumes. Until Desdemona got into her nightgown, you couldn't see what all the fuss was about.

By this time in the production, many of the other actors had grown tired of rehearsing; they had got set in their interpretations and Peter had let them go off in certain directions that formed little cliques onstage. Zoe just rearranged everything. I was happy; I thought, 'This might save the production'; but Dianne, our third Desdemona, had inherited an uncomfortable situation.

As I recall, she observed that she had arrived too late, saying, 'All the love has been burnt out. It's just depressing me too much. I don't have a place in this production.' Before long, she chose to leave.

With my blessing, as our fourth Desdemona Zoe Caldwell cast Cecilia Hart, my wife. I do not want to perpetuate the myth that I marry all my Desdemonas. I fell in love with Ceci long before she played Desdemona to my Othello. We were married after *Othello* opened on Broadway, but before she joined the production. She is an experienced classical actress and won rave reviews for her role in Tom Stoppard's *Dirty Linen* on Broadway. Ceci brought strength as well as grace to her portrayal of Desdemona, and had this to say about the role:

> For the modern actress, the modern woman, Desdemona is a very difficult role to play, or at least it was for me. I found it had to carry that kind of numbskull innocence right to the very moment two and a half hours later when Othello wraps his hands around her throat before she even asks what is wrong.

Kelsey Grammer took over the role of Cassio in the production. Before he was cast in that role, he was buried among the supernumeraries of the production. He was one of the officers and gentlemen standing around in the Duke's court, or on the dock in the bay. In the cases of Brabantio and Cassio in the production, I probably needed men of more weight – literally more weight. I wanted a Brabantio as 'beefy' as I was, and they gave me one, and it worked. I wanted the same thing with Cassio, in a younger form, and they found Kelsey Grammer, who became a dashing and convincing Cassio. Chris had a tendency to move young actors about onstage like chess pieces – and this experience could be an education for young actors like Kelsey. Reflecting on the dynamics of this production, Kelsey told a CBC interviewer that Peter Coe said to him, 'Kelsey, just do whatever Christ tells you.' With his usual humour, Kelsey added that he thought, 'I've been had. I've been had by Captain von Trapp.'

I have said before that Peter Coe and I were star-crossed. Oddly, every time there ever was a conjunction of the energies of Peter Coe and James Earl Jones, there was a disaster that Nostradamus would have been proud to have predicted. If we had been planets, we would have been in opposite spheres, and in danger of collision. Whenever one of us entered the other's sphere, there was sometimes friction between us, and always disaster beyond us. It seemed to extend beyond the theatre. When we did *Next Time I'll Sing for You*, and were about to go into previews. I had taken a lunch break that day when I heard the terrible news that John F. Kennedy had been murdered. Peter, with some grace, dismissed the company to mourn.

Years later, when I flew to New York to complete the arrangements to begin working with Peter on this *Othello*, even as I was signing the contract, I heard the news that Ronald Reagan had been the victim of an attempted assassination. I guess Peter and I should have known by then that we had best avoid each other.

I have always thought that this production attempted in vain to combine the cynical comedy from Iago with the tragedy of Othello. That, though, was not the director's vision of the play; it just happened that way. Despite my misgivings, however, the play was a big hit on Broadway, perhaps because of its perversity. Certainly Chris's performance contributed to the popularity of the production. Audiences loved it despite, or perhaps even because of, the cynicism – onstage and offstage. Chris received a Tony nomination for best actor in 1982, and the play won the Tony for best revival of a drama. This was a significant recognition for our producers, Barry and Fran Weissler, for *Othello* was their first Broadway show, and the Tony was their first major award. It launched them in the big league of Broadway producers, and they have been there ever since.

It was Hamlet who said of drama, 'Give me a platform and a passion or two.' That's the fundamental formula for a play: a space you fill with the words that not only depict but also evoke passions. Sir Tyrone Guthrie said that, for playwrights, the play as seen on the page is only the tip of an iceberg. In a good play, what is underneath the surface is integral to how the tip of the iceberg is formed. There is more substance below the surface, and the author himself is often not aware of what he has put together. If the play is well written, there should be some mysteries to the author as well. A well-crafted piece has that in its nature: the text is less than absolute; there is more to it; it is a guide to all that is underneath the surface.

How do the director and the actors make the play work? Quite often, they first acknowledge the text, explore every line, and dig below the surface. The director then has the challenge of establishing the vision of the play and casting the characters.

Once, in New York, I heard a lecture by the actor and director George Devine of the Royal Court Theatre. (He was one of a group who took over the Royal Court in 1956, and he became its director. Under his leadership, the Royal Court fostered the work of playwrights such as John Osborne and actors such as Albert Finney and Nicol Williamson.) Devine quickly got our attention as actors when he said, in effect, 'All you need is a play and a bunch of actors. Directors can be useful, but they are not necessary. Producers can be useful, but they aren't necessary. But you do need actors and you need a play. That's really all you need.'

This gives credence to George C. Scott's naughty suggestion that we cast everybody – including the producer and the director. They should be cast to make sure we have the right people to help realize the production and to make sure that we actors stay on track.

The producer has to make certain crucial decisions, such as whether to offer a full costume production. He or she needs the wisdom to understand that, when you transfer a play into another time period, you encounter problems that you may not be able to solve as a producer. If you can't solve them, you leave your actors and directors at risk. Because the producer has to be accountable for that kind of decision, he or she must be sure that the play is well cast.

To be valuable to the production, the director has to be accountable in making sure that all the people, including the actors and the technicians, have the same dramatic vision in mind. This is not so much for interpretation, because interpretation will grow, evolve and vary from the first rehearsal to the final production.

As part of that vision, the director brings the actors and the audience into the mores of the time. It is important for the director and the actors to examine the culture of the play's time and place. Then you find the consensus about what was thought of Moors, what was thought of Turks, what was thought of women, and of all other key elements of the play. Much of *Othello* is about military combat and the director has to take us into an awareness of how that combat is different from today, and how the act of heroism is different.

Drama critic Harold Clurman wrote, 'Othello is a part very few actors have succeeded in portraying successfully. That is why the flashier part of Iago, which requires mere skill and personality, is usually sought by stars and applauded by audiences. The part of Othello is so physically and emotionally demanding that Stanislavsky once said no actor could to it justice more than twice a week . . .'[*]

I think Shakespearean actors do need to be strong, stalwart people to sustain the physical and emotional demands of the plays. Just as Shakespeare is the height and the best we have in terms of language, we should have Shakespearean actors who are the height and the best in terms of physical specimens – handsome people with good, strong voices. For the stage especially, one hopes to see people who have not only the physical but also the emotional strength to plumb the depths of the play. Actors must be willing to dive below the surface in order to create the richest, fullest performance for the audience to witness on the stage.

[*] Harold Clurman, *Lies Like Truth: Theatre Reviews and Essays* (New York: The Macmillan Company, 1958), 155–6.

A Dozen or So Other Journeys Worth Noting

DESDEMONA
What wouldst thou write of me, if thou shouldst praise me?
IAGO
O gentle lady; do not put me to't,
For I am nothing, if not critical.
(Act II, scene i)

Ever since Shakespeare wrote *Othello*, some time between 1601 and 1604, actors, directors, audience members and scholars have been trying to parse the text and decipher the characters and themes of the play. Like me, for various reasons, some people take the drama too personally. Some people cannot accept it merely as a story. Some people are troubled by certain characters, or by certain questions: did Othello and Desdemona consummate their marriage? How could Desdemona appear to die and then speak again? Why was Othello so vulnerable to Iago's 'temptations'? What really motivates Iago? What, if anything, was Shakespeare saying about jealousy, marriage, the place of women in society, conflicting cultures, race, war, good and evil?

Many generations of pundits have devoted years, if not whole careers, to exploring the endlessly rich and fascinating worlds of Shakespeare's drama. They, too, take *Othello* and the other plays very personally. One hopes that all study of Shakespeare, whether literary study or dramaturgical study and performance, has as its purpose the illumination of the plays; but I think there is a danger both in subjectively embracing the play and in objectively dissecting it. This warning was issued in 1865 by the Reverend William R. Arrowsmith, author of *Shakespeare's Editors and Commentators*:

> Let but Iago say that for soldiership his comrade Cassio is 'a fellow almost damned in a fair wife' – that his qualifications for the post of lieutenant would be almost discreditable in a woman; let him add withal, as though on set purpose to preclude every chance of being misunderstood, that Cassio possesses no more strategic knowledge than a 'spinster', when lo! a goodly troop of commentators, clerk and lay, bishop and bookseller, lawyer and antiquary, critic professional and critic amateur, homeborn and outlandish, men who have read much and men who have read nothing, swarm forth to bury this simple remark under a pile of notes, that from first to last contain not an inkling of its purport . . . *

At times, Shakespearean editors have to be cryptologists, trying to figure out codes. They can generate a 'pile of notes' about a play that can leave us without 'an inkling of its purport'. Sometimes they seem to be advancing an agenda that has little to do with the play itself; but they can also lead us to information or interpretations that can be valuable and illuminating. The 'pile of notes' can often be fun, and can enrich our knowledge of the plays.

I have found several texts to be especially helpful, and this book contains the bibliographical details. For me, the following volumes stay close by on the Shakespeare bookshelf:

First, there is Horace Howard Furness's *Othello: The New Variorum Edition*, published in 1886, but fortunately made

---

* The Reverend W. R. Arrowsmith, *Shakespeare's Editors and Commentators* (London: J. Russell Smith, 1865) 38, quoted in Horace Furness, 9.

available in a paperback reprint in 2000. I think this is the richest *Othello* text available, because it gives us comprehensive annotation and an extensive overview of references and scholarly and dramaturgical interpretations.

Harold C. Goddard's two-volume *The Meaning of Shakespeare* comes next in value for me. Goddard gives us the most *balanced* understanding of the characters, taking them all at their best. That is important to give the play its richest, most balanced, potential interpretation.

Every author other than Furness and Goddard had an agenda for writing about the play. The agendas often get in the way, and they rarely have to do with putting the play onstage to work in front of an audience. It is helpful to read with that in mind.*

One of Shakespeare's most controversial critics was also one of the earliest, Thomas Rymer. In *A Short View of Tragedy*, in 1693, he described *Othello* as 'a bloody farce without salt or savour'. He so aggressively attacked this play in particular, and Shakespeare's tragedies in general, that he has been called a fanatic and a tyrant. To some, Rymer has seemed to be the best critic who ever lived, and to others, the worst.

Helen Nowak's translation of *Stanislavski Produces Othello* is of great value for directors and actors, and does not deal just with the method acting of the play. In fact, the book points out the danger of approaching the play with emotions you can barely hear or understand: those deep Marlon Brando, Jimmy Dean feelings. Stanislavski cautions against using what he called 'temperament'. He says that if what comes out of your mouth comes only from your understanding of the character's feelings for the moment, it won't sustain you. The poetry of the play demands something much larger and much more

* Perhaps Goddard did have an agenda, but if so, it is so similar to mine that I don't mind a bit.

sustained than that. The gist of what Stanislavski was getting at is almost counter-method, or perhaps 'method-plus'.

He tells the interesting story of the actor Tommaso Salvini, who was a great, if controversial, Othello. Salvini spoke no English or Russian. He did his Othello in Italian; the rest of the cast spoke English, and it didn't matter. What mattered was what was evoked on stage. Othello rarely gets rough beyond threats with anybody, in most productions, but in the moment when he challenges Iago to give him proof of Desdemona's alleged infidelity, Salvini threw the actor playing Iago to the ground and raised his foot to stomp him. Stanislavski says that the audience stood up, as if they believed Salvini/Othello was going to kill Iago with his foot; the actor's passion infused the scene with that degree of reality. Stanislavski suggests that, once you find such a gesture and fill the gesture with your passion, the play can take on new power.

In his book *Acting Shakespeare* Bertram Joseph speaks helpfully of the way an actor can get in touch with the poetry of the play without going the route that some American actors are taught and some British actors use from childhood: being so exceedingly and distractingly aware of the beauty of the language that the sound sometimes overwhelms the meaning. Shakespeare's plays *are* about the beauty of the language, of course, but Joseph writes that there is an inherent beauty in the language that you can discover no matter what cultural accent you have.

He mentions, for instance, the onomatopoeia in *Henry V*, specifically in the use of the word 'mock'. The gauntlet is laid down, and King Henry and the King of France challenge each other to a battle. The French send back a box of tennis balls as a way of saying, 'Up yours. This is going to be a tennis match for us.' In response, Henry plays on the word 'mock' in the face of this 'mock' threat. The word 'mock' becomes the sound of the strike against the ball, and the rally goes on for quite a while. When it is recited properly, it sounds as if Henry is mocking a tennis match. The onomatopoeia is a lively illustration of Shakespeare's organic use of poetry. King Henry V says,

> And tell the pleasant prince this mock of his
> Hath turn'd his balls to gun-stones; and his soul
> Shall stand sore charged for the wasteful vengeance
> That shall fly with them; for many a thousand widows
> Shall this his mock mock out of their dear husbands;
> Mock mothers from their sons, mock castles down . . .
> (*King Henry V*, Act I, scene ii)

Many commentaries on Shakespeare are not about putting the play onstage; they are about putting forward certain concepts of the play. Harold Bloom's *Shakespeare: The Invention of the Human* offers right up front something that many other writers don't say. When you divide the play between the good guys and the bad guys, the bad guys have the running start in *Othello*. You don't know who Othello is or who Desdemona is until they have been vilified or until they are in the thick of a conflict. Iago and Rodrigo have the initial scene, and that gives them a running start.

Stage Productions

As the play moves from the page to the stage, there are countless productions to consider, and the best and even the worst of them can teach us valuable lessons about *Othello*. As I have said, I think that women who have directed this play have had a better chance of understanding the cultural sentiments of the drama. I think that's why Margaret Webster made the Paul Robeson–Uta Hagen–Jose Ferrer performances the most realized production of *Othello* of modern times, and I believe Paul Robeson's Othello is the landmark performance of the twentieth century. As a woman, Margaret Webster could understand the issue of jealousy and, even more than that, could understand Desdemona's role in the play better than any man could. The director Gladys Vaughan was the reason our production of *Othello* in Central Park came as close to fruition as it did.

In addition to Margaret Webster's production, I find several worth noting. I've heard stories, of course, about legendary Ira Aldridge, the nineteenth-century African-American actor who first played Othello at the Theatre Royal in Covent Garden in London in 1833, and was hailed as a star of the first magnitude.

Of twentieth-century Othellos, Earle Hyman did a production at the Riverside Church just as I arrived in New York in 1958, but I didn't have a chance to see it. It was always considered the bridge between the Robeson work and any future work done by African-American actors in *Othello*. Moses Gunn did a performance on Broadway in 1968. It was a notable portrayal because he gave us an Othello who was really a superior human being in his own attitude. He treated the world as if he was superior. That is not exactly the choice I would recommend, but it won notable reviews because Othello literally looked down his nose at those around him. If anything, that might have made it more difficult for Othello to make that turn in the road when he is crippled by the confusion about his wife.

I don't think the Iago was fulfilled in that performance. He had no particular qualities that I think are important for Iago. Iago is most effective when he behaves like Satan but looks like Lucifer. He should be a gorgeous presence on stage. Errol John's 1964 British stage production cast Leo McKern as Iago.

McKern was a rotund, barrel-chested man who had no truck with glamour at all. His was a very interesting, very aggressive interpretation. He was not the reason the play failed.

Raul Julia played Othello to Christopher Walken's Iago in a production in the Delacorte Theater in Central Park in 1991. This rendition suffered from the bulldog-and-the-bear syndrome. More recently, a British production at the Brooklyn Academy of Music offered an Iago who conceived himself as a toad. He took literally the conception that Cassio's beauty made Iago ugly. He had been cheated out of life not only by Othello but by God. It was intriguing to watch, although it didn't resolve the problems that Iago presents; but it almost worked.

This production gave us a young, strapping, strong Othello, suggesting that the romance does not have to be a May–September relationship. This casting results in a kind of counterpoint to the May–September romance, such as the one involving the actor Walter Huston as Governor Peter Minuit in the 1938 Broadway show *Knickerbocker Holiday*. (Huston made a hit with his rendition of 'September Song'.)

A 2001 Public Theater performance in New York starred Liev Schreiber as Iago and Keith David as Othello. The prelude of that production was an article Liev wrote for the *New York Times* about how the events of 11 September 2001 affected his view of the play. The article was just a mind trip for the reader, and alerted us to what Liev might do with the performance. What the performance did was give us something akin to a farce within a play. It so isolated the Iago moments that it resolved what the other actors do on the stage when Iago is expressing his machinations. A stab of sound and a blast of light isolated Iago almost as if an alien spaceship had beamed him up. He functioned in that isolated world – that's what I call the farce of the play – but Liev could misbehave as much as he wanted to. This almost upstaged the tragedy, and left it as a backdrop.

If all else is failing – if Desdemona is not up to snuff; if Othello is played as a boring fool – then for the sake of the producer's penny, Iago had certainly better strike out and give the audience the entertainment they paid for. I have heard of a production where Othello carries a midget Iago about on his shoulders, suggesting a weird alter-ego situation. I myself was encouraged by Tad Danielewski to do a film production where I would play both Othello and Iago, or a production to explore the father–son mythology between Othello and Iago. (Who is the father and who is the son?) The Juilliard School of Drama mounted a production in which both Othello and Iago were black, and other ethnic mixes have been tried. Some of these ideas are tempting and exciting, but none, I believe, is as exciting as playing the play straight and true – as far as we can determine what is straight and true in the text. After all, it's just theatre. It's just show business. Try anything you want; but none of it can be as exciting as the straight play.

Motion Pictures

Fortunately, since 1908 there have been some interesting, provocative productions of *Othello* on film. Orson Welles's 1952 screen adaptation is one of the most notable. The film won the top award at the 1952 Cannes Film Festival, but was not well received when it opened in the United States in 1955. With the leadership of Welles's daughter, the film was restored and shown in movie theatres again in 1992.

Welles's cinematic genius gave us a wonderful visual production. The film opens with stunning gothic, black-and-white images of the funeral procession of the tragic figures, Othello, Desdemona and Emilia. This parade of the dead is set against the winching aloft of Iago confined in a torture cage, which echoes Gratiano's words: 'Torments will ope your lips' (Act V, scene ii). So the Welles adaptation immediately confronts us with the funeral procession, and the torture of Iago.

The opening narration borrows heavily from Cinthio, and we are informed that this is a motion-picture adaptation of *The Tragedy of Othello, the Moor of Venice* by William Shakespeare. This adaptation ends up being only a wonderful trailer for the play *Othello*. We are given just snatches of Shakespeare's dialogue, and it tries to lay a track of events and intentions, of people's positions and motivations. Some of this compression and distillation is very effective, but even so, we are, in a way, denied Shakespeare.

We become aware of these snatches of dialogue when the relationship of Roderigo and Iago is first presented to us, and many of these truncated lines are totally out of sequence. Iago is not only completely incredible, but, I believe, disturbingly badly cast. He is played by Michael MacLiammoir, a man with a fine sense of humour and great wit. Welles and MacLiammoir enjoyed a wonderful relationship in the Gate Theatre of Dublin. (In fact, they both had the great pleasure of riding into town on their asses, a tradition for actors joining the theatre in Dublin. MacLiammoir wrote a book called *Every Actor on His Ass*.) Orson Welles was the only actor in this production with the training, ability and talent for film characterization. Everyone else was doing stage work at best, and therefore their film performances were not even notable.

MacLiammoir gave us an Iago who was totally unacceptable. Although he is used as a guide for tracking the imagery of the story, he is someone you wouldn't want around you. He is a simpering, Machiavellian figure who is totally disturbing in the wrong way. Not only would you not believe this man, or want him in your company, he is a pariah. He drips with more than malevolence – with the ills of humanity. I don't understand how this Iago could hold this rank in Othello's cadre.

Welles was the only person in the film who fulfilled Shakespeare's vision, and he fulfilled it beautifully. He gives us a sad, almost morose Moor, and you can see the vulnerable Little Otto, the saddest little boy. Desdemona was achieved by several actresses, owing to the sporadic filming process: Welles would film until he ran out of money, and then stop to earn more. In fact, he made *The Third Man* during one of these interludes. When he had earned the funds to resume filming, an actress might not be available, and he would recast, but it didn't matter because Desdemona is not explored anyway.

The little bit of dialogue she is given to utter only exaggerates her victimhood. She acquits herself very well in her truncated Senate speech and at other moments, but for the most part she is a victim, and vulnerable, which is a great misfortune.

The first extended speech from Shakespeare that Welles gives us is the Senate speech where Othello defends his marriage. The interpretation is wonderful. You see an Othello very different from Sir Laurence Olivier's. There is no conceit or affectation. He is very pure.

At one point, I thought the Welles film might help me track a road map to show how characters move from point to point in the drama. However, I need more of a road map than this wonderful 'trailer' gives me. The truncated speeches, the cuts and edits of language and action result in an abrupt turnabout in Othello. All of a sudden, without proper preparation, he veers from joyful husband to the confused man vulnerable to jealousy. This is always the case if you aren't careful how you build up to this change. Much depends on how credible Iago is. This adaptation gives us an Othello who is suddenly jealous because of someone else's words and suggestions. It leaves him oddly weakened and a bit foolish.

So the Welles production does not assuage the old fear of Othello being a dupe.

However, Welles with his genius is able to take us through labyrinthine scenes and sets. The winding staircases begin to have the effect of spiralling human passions and behaviour, right through to the end. This serves in a way to lead us to Othello's seizure, because the camera propels us, swirls us, spirals us into his descent into epilepsy and madness.

It's quite clear from Welles's interpretation of Othello that he is not resolved as being jealous. He is bitten; he will never sleep again; but he is only profoundly confused. I think Shakespeare's dialogue bears that out, and Welles is faithful to it.

The handkerchief scene is dealt with very simply in an isolated scene. We see Othello and Desdemona lose the handkerchief. We cut to another scene and we see Emilia discover it, so her implication in the responsibility over the handkerchief is not as bad. Because of the set – the seashore, battlements – when Othello is threatening Iago to prove that Desdemona is a whore, he simply has Iago on a wall and threatens to do him over. All these visual effects are compelling.

After the seizure, when Othello revives himself, he questions, 'Dost thou mock me?' (Act IV, scene i). This is very well done. There is no explanation – just one cut of Othello asking the question. His subsequent line: '. . . a fine woman, a fair woman, a sweet woman!' clearly expresses confusion, not jealousy. When we get to: 'Had it pleas'd heaven . . .' (Act IV, scene ii), the film conveys the concept I've been harping on. Othello touches Desdemona's body when he speaks of the fountain from which his current runs. I think, 'Yes! Someone else agrees with me on that.'

At the end of this scene, when Othello says, 'I took you for that cunning whore of Venice / That married with Othello,' Desdemona is played as if in catatonic shock. Not only that, but she is resigned. The effect is quite stunning.

Welles achieves another intriguing effect through serendipity. Because the props and the set had not arrived by the time he was ready to film the assassination of Cassio, he used a steam house. It is very interesting. Toward the end, Iago's attempt to stab Roderigo through the slats foreshadows his imprisonment in the torture cage.

When Desdemona asks Emilia if she thinks there are women who abuse their husbands, Emilia answers, 'There be some such, no question' (Act IV, scene iii). Then she delivers her lines in good Susan B. Anthony style, as a charmless, very sophisticated, non-woman, non-citizen. The dawning of Emilia's realization that it is her own husband who caused all this chaos is very interesting. My wife has awakened my curiosity about whether Emilia really loves Iago, so that when it dawns on her, it is as much a shock to her as it is to anyone in the whole play.

As Welles delivers the farewell speech – the one that often is declared to be an indulgence in megalomania – it is simply a pure soliloquy, not even a personal one. He is reflecting on his whole life. He simply makes a statement: 'It is gone.' 'Othello's occupation's gone' (Act III, scene iii). Welles begins with: 'Farewell the tranquil mind' (Act III, scene iii), and that's the point: Othello's tranquil mind is gone. He states it very simply.

Othello's suicide, the fatal blow, comes very early. It is not even telegraphed, but he stabs himself long before he dies. The whole final scene is collapsed upon itself very effectively. When Othello finally succumbs to his suicidal stabbing, he looks up through a hatch, and he says, 'When you shall these unlucky deeds relate, / Speak of me as I am.' He collapses on the bed, dead, and we cut to the procession that opened the film. The effect is stunning. I think this film is well worth any director or any cast viewing, certainly for visual impact and for how to fulfil the story in space.

Welles, though, is the only actor in the film with any film presence. His acting is natural; it's modern. He really knows what he's doing. I've heard that Welles never allowed any on-set dialogue to be used. He would go into the privacy of the sound stage and redo his own dialogue. I don't know if he did it here, but it's worth exploring.

Sir Laurence Olivier's film version of *Othello* appeared in 1965. Frank Finlay played a cynical Iago, a surly, contemptible, callow fellow who sneers at us way past the point of what would have been grounds for dismissal in the military. Olivier gives us a giddy, giggly Othello at the outset, although he later plays him with great authority, thereby growing more credible. Brabantio is well played, rattled rather than judgemental, a man in the throes of tremendous fear.

In the Venice scenes of the play, Othello stands as the dynamic centre, the sun around which all the other planets revolve, including the Duke. On Cyprus, Desdemona becomes the sun. Iago is played as a crusty villain, confiding in – or confessing to – the audience. If Iago were confessing this way to a priest, I think the priest would say, 'I don't believe you. You are making an appeal to absolve yourself of sin. I want you to give me your confession straight and pure. Don't try to bullshit anybody, especially God.' I think the priest would recommend therapy rather than beads to this Iago. Emilia is played as if she is in the middle of a car wreck and not aware of it, or even caring about it. Desdemona has one redeeming moment in the willow scene, and she comes in like a fresh breeze at that point.

Eventually, however, Olivier's film becomes a solo opera for Othello, as if he is acting all by himself. He does not connect with the other actors. He takes refuge in self-pity. While cuts and deletions are sometimes necessary in a production of any Shakespearean play, I think the text was badly edited here.

Olivier and his company were violating the music of the text. There is hysteria more than confusion and grief, and cockiness more than the grandeur of life; and I wanted to wipe off the makeup by then!

I have never seen a more profound derailment of a potentially wonderful production. The drama's whole spine collapses with this approach. The play spins into something perverse. I attribute part of the problem to the difficulty of transferring a stage play to film. Techniques and gestures that work beautifully onstage can fail on film.

On the film, close up, we do not see Olivier going for the tears. We see a technical performance of a man crying. Othello should never be caught acting. I think it was Olivier who said to a young actor, 'You're an actor? Don't let anybody ever catch you at it.' In this film, Olivier violated one of his most famous admonitions; but it is difficult to move from stage to film. I know because I had the same experience with *The Great White Hope*. After playing a role onstage for months, an actor develops certain habits of behaviour that are hard to break down in order to work effectively in a motion picture.

The 1995 *Othello* with Laurence (Larry) Fishburne as Othello and Kenneth Branagh as Iago was filmed at a fifteenth-century castle near Rome. Iago's soliloquies are delivered straight into the camera. Larry Fishburne seemed to be reaching for an Othello that was more sinister than Iago. Kenneth Branagh seemed oddly detached and removed, perhaps because he was also the director.

Television

One of the most recent television films inspired by *Othello* is a modern dress adaptation broadcast in 2001 by Canadian

Broadcast Company (CBC), LWT, and, in the United States, by WGBH, the Public Television affiliate in Boston, Massachusetts. Here we had a chance to enjoy the play without the 'burden' of Shakespeare's dialogue; but that freedom allowed certain things to be touched on – the epilepsy in particular.

Right away, it is revealed to us that there is something – not rotten in the state of Denmark, but corrupt at the core of the city state. John Othello (well played by Eamonn Walker) and Desdemona get married against the stormy backdrop of rioting and racism. Iago, or Ben Jago, is drowning in this turbulence – a predator fish working everybody else in the only water he knows.

Unfortunately, Jago/Iago and his director seem to have a need to play outside the loop, to peek beyond the camera to us, the audience, and to flirt with us. As I have indicated, this is a great temptation to many actors playing Iago and I think it's wrong. Iago needs to soliloquize – to leave us alone and do his job. The director needs to be quite clear that a soliloquy is not a wink at the audience, but a character's conversation with his own psyche, his own conscience or godhead.

Desdemona and Emilia are the same age in this production, good 'jet-setting' friends, and Iago and Othello are the same level or rank in the police hierarchy. Iago's motivation is now heightened because he and Othello are equal in rank, but Othello receives the promotion because of his colour – the diplomatic thing for the Prime Minister to do. When Iago gets the news, he says to Othello, almost endearingly, 'You clever black bastard!' It's the first time Iago has mentioned colour, and colour begins to work against Othello in his fall. Iago loses control as the play progresses. He has his own 'epileptic fit'. In this modern version of the play Othello gives us almost an African-American awareness of race. It is suggested that he is 'Mr Victim', who wishes he had been white when he was a kid. Iago also gives Othello a second affliction: impotence.

Finally, Iago seems as unattractive as he says Cassio makes him, with a classic lean and hungry look. Iago acknowledges that events have spiraled out of his control. He confesses to the audience, 'I wish it hadn't gone this far.'

In 1980 there was the Anthony Hopkins/Bob Hoskins production of *Othello* on BBC television, part of the plan to do all the Shakespeare plays. I was in the back story of that production, as I was eligible to compete for the leading role. Anthony Quayle was in the United States at the time, and was going to announce the casting of an American in the role of Othello. Overnight, a decision was made in British Actors Equity in which even the black actors of Britain chimed in and said, 'We don't need an American to play Othello. There are plenty of black British actors who can do that.'

What happened is that no black actor got to play Othello in the BBC production; the role was given to Anthony Hopkins. I don't begrudge that, however, because I was happy when I saw the production not to have been involved with it. It was unfulfilled. Hopkins seemed lost. Hoskins was no more subtle or revealing than Frank Finlay was in the Laurence Olivier production. Hoskins reminded me a lot of Leo McKern – rotund, barrel-chested, brusque, without grace. I thought that left Iago lacking – not to be invested with grace.

I watched all the BBC presentations, and I said to myself, 'If they had given the role of Iago to Alan Rickman, who played Antonio in *Measure for Measure*, and if he had delivered essentially what he did as the villain in *Measure for Measure*, which is a comedy, he probably would have given us the greatest Iago we've ever seen.'

All productions can be valuable. I learned from reviews and the film of Campbell Scott's production of *Hamlet* that, having grown up with his father's work in Shakespeare, and then seen his generation tackling the plays, he wanted to take his own crack at Shakespeare. The whole purpose is for each new generation to take a turn. The goal is not to achieve the definitive production, although that might happen at some time. Our job is to illuminate the production as richly as we are capable of doing. This means we may have to sacrifice pet theories and easy interpretations. We may have to be willing to explore contradictions; and we will need to dive below the surface to discover what lies beneath the crown of the iceberg.

Ultimately, actors and directors have to find their own pathways as they enter the complex world of this play. Likewise, all the people who sit in the darkened theatre to experience the play must discover it on their own, as if it were the first time. Each generation takes up the discovery anew.

With *The Tragedy of Othello, the Moor of Venice*, we embrace a great challenge. It will always be there. It will never go away. That bears out Tyrone Guthrie's theory about what is under the tip of the iceberg.

It is eternity.

Readings about *Othello*: A Brief Annotated Bibliography

Harold Bloom, *Shakespeare: The Invention of the Human*
(New York: Riverhead Books, 1998)
Bloom says that this is Othello's tragedy, 'even if it is Iago's play'. He says that only *Othello* and *Coriolanus* exclude all laughter, as if to 'protect two great captains from the Falstaffian perspective' (434). Bloom is saying it is all right to think of Falstaff as a fool, because Shakespeare was using him for some enlightening humour; but in no way was he using the character Othello for humour.

Charles N. Coe, *Shakespeare's Villains* (New York: Bookman, 1957)
This book compares Iago and Aaron the Moor in *Titus Andronicus*. The scholar seems to think that everything Iago says is true.

Leslie A. Fiedler, *The Stranger in Shakespeare* (London: Croom Helm, 1973)
Fiedler examines the Moor as a stranger, and suggests that Shakespeare's plays can teach us about how modern society treats the stranger or the outsider, and about the roots of racism and sexism. He sees *Othello* as a one-act comedy followed by a tragedy in four acts.

Harold C. Goddard, *The Meaning of Shakespeare* (Chicago and London: The University of Chicago Press, 1951 and 1960)
I think this is the largest, richest, most wholesome treatment of *Othello*.

Bertram Joseph, *Acting Shakespeare* (New York: Theatre Arts Books, 1981)
This book is valuable for actors, directors and general readers because of its emphasis on the meanings embedded in the text of the play.

Helen Nowak, translator, *Stanislavski Produces Othello* (New York: Theatre Arts Books, 1948; 1968)
Stanislavski writes: 'Why should Iago wish for this part [the promotion]? He is an intimate friend as it is; he is a friend of the house; he belongs. Let him stay where he is . . .' (18).

Eric Partridge and Stanley Wells, *Shakespeare's Bawdy* (London and New York: Routledge, 2001)
This book is meant to be light, but it also deals with some of the harder issues.

Marvin Rosenberg, *The Masks of Othello: The Search for the Identity of Othello, Iago, and Desdemona by Three Centuries of Actors and Critics* (Newark: University of Delaware Press, n.d.)
The chapter called 'In Defense of Iago' says that Shakespeare shaped Iago into 'a first-rate dramatic personality . . .' (167). An argument is made that you have to look into Iago's inner life, because Shakespeare 'understood and dramatized the hidden working of the soul' (173).

A. P. Rossiter, *Angel with Horns and Other Shakespeare Lectures* (New York: Theatre Arts Books/Longmans, Green & Co., Ltd., 1961)
Rossiter says that you have to consider the bloody farce. He deals with plays on the outlands of the category of comedy.

Bernard Spivack, *Shakespeare and the Allegory of Evil: The History of a Metaphor in Relation to His Major Villains* (New York: Columbia University Press, 1958)

The book is so scholarly that I have a hard time wading through it and finding anything that makes sense to me. But it's such a grand title, I don't want to throw it out!